THE TANGLED GARDEN

Memories of my Girlhood

THE
TANGLED GARDEN

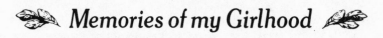 *Memories of my Girlhood*

ELIZABETH COLEMAN

LONDON
VICTOR GOLLANCZ LTD
1988

First published in Great Britain in 1988
by Victor Gollancz Limited
14 Henrietta Street, London WC2E 8QJ

British Library Cataloguing in Publication Data
Coleman, Elizabeth
    The tangled garden : memories of my girlhood.
    1. Country Life — England   2. England —
    Social life and customs — 20th century
    I. Title
    942.083'092'4   DA589.4

ISBN 0-575-04187-0

Typeset at The Spartan Press Ltd,
Lymington, Hants
and printed in Great Britain by
St Edmundsbury Press Ltd, Bury St Edmunds, Suffolk

My book
is dedicated to
Mrs K. Lathbury
without whose help
it might never have been published

I

"Now you have given me all this work, see you stick in this job, my girl," my mother said. For two weeks she had been busy making cotton dresses, caps and aprons for me to go into my first situation as a live-in maid. I was just fifteen years old.

I was the youngest of a family of five children — three brothers who had all left home and whom I hardly ever saw, and my sister Rachel who was much older than I and now married with a growing daughter. My father worked in the coal mines. I had left school when I was thirteen-and-a-half and got a job cleaning and washing dishes for a family about half an hour's walk away from our home in Abercynon. But not long after, in 1914, war had broken out and the men of that family had volunteered, and Mrs Saunders, my mistress, had given up the house and moved to Bristol.

My new situation was in Penarth, a train journey of fifteen miles away from home and I arrived there in a state of some trepidation. I was very nervous. I was shown to a small bedroom right at the top of the house. This I was to share with the other maid, who was much older than I — about thirty.

"When you have changed, and put your black dress on — and for goodness' sake, pin your hair up, you can't have your hair round your neck like that — you can find your way down to the kitchen. The missus will see you then." I found my way down the three flights of stairs. Mrs Pettigrew, the mistress, was waiting for me. She looked me over.

"Oh yes, you look quite smart, you'll have to answer the door to visitors when Aggie is away. She has been very good, and we have been without a second maid for quite a while, so I must let her off a little more now to make up for it." She was

Scottish, a tall woman of about sixty with grey hair; she looked very aristocratic and rather forbidding. I felt awed. She gave me the feeling that I must only speak when spoken to, and there would be no warmth there.

"You will get up at five-thirty in the morning with Aggie, come down the stairs very, very quietly. You must be down by six o'clock, washed and dressed. You will have the kitchen to scrub and the hall to scrub (the hall and kitchen were tiled) before breakfast. There will be dishes to wash and vegetables to clean after breakfast. Aggie will be on the bedrooms. Prayers will be at ten in the morning-room, which you and Aggie must attend. That will be all for now." She turned to Aggie, "I must get some food for Elizabeth." Away she went, and later came back with a number of packages. "Usually I give out your food on Monday mornings, but today is Wednesday. This should be enough until Monday."

When she left the room I looked on as Aggie unwrapped them and I felt a bit shaken: a quarter of a pound of margarine, about two ounces of cheese, a handleless cup with about two dessertspoons of jam, two rashers of bacon, one egg, about six ounces of sugar. I had never been doled out with 'rations' before, I had never been away from home before, and I didn't know what to expect, but I was shattered to think that I had to live on this for four or five days.

We worked from six in the morning until ten at night when the mistress came to tell us to go to bed. By the time I had finished scrubbing the large kitchen and hall I was starving. We had no cup of tea on getting up in the morning. Servants were not indulged or fussed over. You were just there as a cog in a wheel that had to keep turning. Breakfast was either porridge or the bacon and egg we had been given. We were allowed half an hour for each meal. There was the silver and the brass to clean and the furniture to polish. At ten we trooped in for morning prayers with Mrs Pettigrew, her daughter and mother-in-law. Aggie spoke little and I was afraid to tell her how I felt in case she might repeat it to the mistress. I found our dinner at one o'clock was made up of vegetables left over from the day before with a cut off the joint in the dining room, which Aggie went to collect when the bell rang. Cooking for the family was not done in our kitchen, but in a separate one, so that there was no heating of any kind. The last meal of the day was our tea at six o'clock, out of the 'rations' we had been given.

I was allowed to go to church on Sunday morning and Sunday evening. Otherwise I was allowed nowhere, and for the six months I was there I went into Penarth only once. That was when I developed a bad finger and I was told to go to a chemist's to have it seen to. I went home to see my mother twice during that time, and was sent off in time to get the train and was told to be back on a certain train while it was still daylight. Later I found out that my father had written to Mrs Pettigrew to say that I should not be allowed out too much. She had acted accordingly. I am sure I would have had more freedom if it had not been for my father's letter, freedom to see the place I lived in: I would have liked to have gone down to the beach.

I was preparing to go to church one Sunday morning. My hair being short and curly looked ridiculous in the little tight bun I had had to screw it up into while on duty, but as I was going to church I dressed it my own way — in curls that spread loosely about the back of my hat. I was late in getting to church, Miss Pettigrew and her father were already seated in church, and must have seen me arrive. After church I followed an impulse to see what it looked like up the road, at least a little way from the Pettigrews' house, so by the time I arrived home the daughter and father were already there.

I went into the kitchen prior to going upstairs to change into my uniform, and Aggie gave me a message. "Before you go upstairs you are to go into the drawing room, the mistress wishes to see you just as you are." I went, and the mistress sat staring at me for about a minute.

"You must not go to church again with your hair dressed that way. It makes you look like a schoolgirl. You will dress your hair just as you do on duty," she said.

I looked at her as she said this, and wondered if for thirteen

9

and sixpence per calendar month she had bought me entirely — it seemed she had, for fourteen and a half hours a day, except for the brief respite I had to go to church. I thought this woman who made her two maids come in to her morning room every day and stand while she read a short piece out of the Bible and then prayed for all of us, for 'God's glory and kindness to us for the day before us,' this woman, what sort of a Christian was she, and in that moment I hated her.

"Madam, while I am on duty I am willing to screw my hair up in a bun, seeing I can do it no other way, although it makes me look silly — but when I go out and it seems I am allowed out only to go to church, I will go out and be myself and look like myself for that time. I look like a schoolgirl, yes, because I am only fifteen."

I was shocked at myself for daring to speak up so, and stood silent and flushed, staring back at her. But if I was shocked so was she. She slowly rose from her chair and said, "Go now to your room and change and see that you are downstairs in a quarter of an hour, and furthermore, you will not do your hair in that ridiculous style again."

I left the room and did as I was told. But next time I went to church my hair was done my way, not as I had been directed, and she said not a word.

The climax came one Sunday. Aggie was away for the day. She had left quite early and I had not been able to go to church for morning service. Lunchtime came. I had been made to prepare vegetables for lunch, but when I was given my meal my vegetables were fried-up cabbage and potatoes left over from the previous day. I left it on the table. When the mistress came out after half an hour and saw my lunch, by now cold, still uneaten, she asked why I had not eaten it. I told her that my father had a family of five children but we had a freshly cooked dinner every day, that I had been with her now for five months and in that time had probably had a freshly cooked dinner about six times in all. "But," I told her, "please don't bother, please take my notice. I will leave you a month from tomorrow."

Mrs Pettigrew wrote to my parents and told them of this; my father wrote to me and told me that both he and my mother hoped I would consider this most carefully and would stay on. It was about a fortnight later that Aggie mentioned that she had seen a letter from my father to Mrs Pettigrew, telling her I was not to be 'allowed out too much, he was afraid that I might find company that would not be good for me'.

The month that followed passed more happily for me; being allowed out only to go to church worried me little, for soon I would be out of the house and would not have to see either Mrs or Miss Pettigrew again. But I was anxious to get another post, and as I did not go out it was difficult to find one.

When there was only a fortnight to go before I was to leave, Aggie told me she had been talking about me to her sister who worked in a solicitor's house and that they needed a girl of about my age as a mother's help. There were four children to look after. She asked me if I would like to go there, and arrangements were made by post for me to go there the day I left the Pettigrews' house. I was very grateful to Aggie.

Aggie's sister was quite a pleasant girl, the people very nice and the children very well behaved. I found too that I had one evening a week to go out, alternate Sundays, and two hours each evening to rest, sew or read from eight until ten o'clock, when we retired.

But after six months, Mrs Hawkins, the mistress, told me that the family were going to America in about a month's time. She had talked of it on a few occasions and I had not given it much attention as I had not thought she had intended leaving so soon. Mrs Hawkins said it would be best for me to look out for something that suited me during the next month as she would like to see me settled in somewhere before she went, unless I intended to go home for a holiday. While I had been with the Hawkins family I had been home on several occasions by train, which I was able to do easily on my evenings off.

My mother always seemed pleased to see me, but with my father I could not feel at ease, although I did my best to be civil and friendly. But I never slept at home again while my parents lived in that house. After I left Mrs Hawkins, I went to Dr and Mrs Armstrong's in Cardiff.

At the Armstrongs' my working day started at seven a.m. As well as being nurse to two nice little boys — Thomas aged four and little Bernard who was just eighteen months old — I began my day by scrubbing the surgery and the long passage that led from the waiting-room and the waiting-room itself, and of course the day nurseries and the night nursery, and my own room. I was responsible for all the children's laundry, but I did not have to do my own. That was sent out along with the other maid's.

I did not make a very good start there, for soon after I arrived I lost Bernard! Mrs Armstrong had asked me to help Phyllis, the other maid, with spring-cleaning the drawing-room, and to leave the children to play in the nursery. I wasn't very pleased by this but imagine my horror when I returned to the nursery to find only Thomas. We searched the whole house from top to bottom to discover to our dismay the front door wide open and no Bernard. Mrs Armstrong was in hysterics because of the traffic and the trams in the road outside. She rushed outside in her dressing-gown and I ran with her, and together we began a search of the lanes nearby. But there was no sign of Bernard.

In tears, Mrs Armstrong phoned the police-station and gave them a description of what he was dressed in.

"We've got the wee chappie here," the policeman said to our relief, and as soon as Mrs Armstrong was dressed we hastened to the police station on the tram. Bernard was happily playing on the floor with a bunch of keys the policeman had given him. It seems he had gone down the drive, crossed the road amidst all the traffic and found his way into a nursery shed where a workman had found him.

"And a fine nurse, you are, losing one of your children like this," the policeman said to me. But Mrs Armstrong explained what had happened.

And, although the work was hard drudgery, I was very

happy at Mrs Armstrong's. I was appreciated, I got on well with the other maid; I was a good nurse and I loved the little children. I was happy there for two years. Then my world collapsed.

2

My father had spent a lifetime working in the coal mines, but now that he was retiring, he decided that he would like to live in the country, in a small cottage with a bit of ground and keep a few fowls and a pig or two. He wrote to his brother who had a farm near Dilwyn in Herefordshire and told him of his requirements. Very soon my uncle had found him a pretty little cottage with about five acres of ground there.

Father went down to see it, liked it, and a week later bought it and also another small cottage just above the house for £400. He came home well pleased with himself and told my mother to get things packed and arrange a furniture remover to take all our worldly goods to the new house.

Mother was a country girl, bred and born, but now she had no wish to move into the country 'to be buried alive, and go nowhere, and see nobody,' as she put it. She liked the small town in which we lived, she had her friends there, and there she was going to stay. My father was equally determined and, as he had bought the property, had made up his mind to live in it — with, of course, my mother. However, when the day arrived to leave he realised that he was going alone. Mother had promised to send the furniture down to his new house and my father left. Now it seemed doubtful whether even the furniture would come, so my father had arranged to sleep at his brother's house until the furnishing of the cottage had been sorted out, but to spend his days at his own place.

As I have said, my three brothers had grown up and left home; two had married and my brother Richard had gone to work in another town, while my sister Rachel and her husband ran a shop in Maesteg.

As my mother had refused to go to Dilwyn, and as Father

would not have dreamed of looking after himself, he decided that *I* would have to give up my post with the Armstrongs and go to keep house for him. His word was law. I had no alternative but to give in my notice. Mrs Armstrong was very disturbed at me wanting to leave. I was shattered.

A week later I left Cardiff and my father met me at Leominster station. We would not be able to carry my luggage, he said, as we had a long walk before us. My large trunk was left at the station until it could be collected by a friend of my uncle's who had a horse and trap. On a Friday there was only one bus that came out from Leominster to our little village. People who were unfortunate enough to have no horse and trap just had to walk. I decided my medium-sized suitcase must go with me, as my nightdress and things for immediate use were in it.

It was a hot April day, the sun shone brightly and we set out on what was to be a six-mile walk, though I did not know it at the time. My father carried my case for a while, then I would take it, and as we walked Father told me much about the house and the little cottage just above it that he had had to buy, as they were not to be sold separately. Our cottage was called Lower Woodlands, the other one Upper Woodlands. There were two rooms up and down, a sizeable dairy that would come in handy when he had a pig big enough to kill, a large scullery with a boiler in it, handy for washing-day. There was no water laid on, he said, when I asked. Water came from a spout out of the bank, but it was lovely clear water and in plentiful supply. Father said the front of the house was very pretty; a small entrance gate opened on to a cobbled stone path, with a flower garden to one side where I could plant more flowers, and behind that a large garden of about half an acre or more, big enough to grow all the vegetables we would need till planting time came again.

As we walked I noticed the new green leaves on the trees, the hedges all neatly cut, buttercups and daisies in such profusion, and the little cottages dotted along the roadside with neatly kept flower gardens in front. But my thoughts were on my father's house, and my new life there. I had misgivings. I felt I was not going to be happy. I knew my father for a good man, religious, hard-working, and a man who could enjoy a drink and leave it at that. But I had been brought up to fear and obey my parents, and had known little of love or great kindness. True, my brothers and myself had had a good home, inasmuch as we were well fed and decently clothed, but I never remember either of my parents cuddling or kissing us. My father was able to squash any nonsense from us by a mere look. My mother had a fist that she used to great effect. I do not think that I loved either of my parents.

We came in sight of a pretty little inn, the 'Tally-ho'. It was red-brick and on the window-sill were boxes of bright red geraniums. There was a large forecourt and my father explained that, as this inn was on the main road, farmers on their way to market liked to draw up their horse and traps for refreshments. We managed to get a glass of cider there. After we left the inn, my father told me about his brother.

"Your Aunt Lizzie is a teetotaller and goes to chapel every Sunday, and while she knows Ted drinks pretty well of cider, seeing he has always made his own, she would not like to know that your uncle does anything so common as visit a pub," Father chuckled. "She has been to market with him only once. She does not go out a lot, except to the village sometimes, and your cousin Lil takes her to her people, I mean Lil's people, now and then. Your aunt likes to do a bit of shopping then."

We came round the bend of the road and, as we did so, saw a farmer doing his best to drive about ten cows through an open gate on the roadside. "Stop a minute guv'nor, will you?" the man shouted. The cows turned into the field as we were just below the gate. "Thank ye, zur, I'm sure. They usually go in quite good as a rule, but I s'pose even cows 'as to 'ave their awk'ard moments."

We walked on and presently my father said, "In about ten minutes we should get to your cousin Paul's place, I expect Lil will be there, and we'll go to her so as you'll see her, because I've arranged for you to sleep there awhile, until we get sorted out. If your mother doesn't send the stuff for the house soon I shall go up to Wales and see to it myself. Your mother always was contrary."

We turned up a side lane, and after a few minutes' walk glimpsed a sizeable farm house.

"That's Paul's place," said my father.

"I hope she will offer us some tea, do you think she will, Dad? It's getting towards teatime now, isn't it?"

"Hm, she may do, she's pretty tight, is Lil," said my father.

My cousin's wife Lil was a tall, angular woman, very dowdily dressed, with her hair pulled back tightly into a bun. Her skirt was originally black but now it had faded into a shade of green; her blouse was also black and none too clean. She wore no apron. Three little boys of between four and nine played around the fireplace, but stopped to stare at my father and me. Lil said, 'How do you do?' when my father introduced us, but made no attempt to shake hands.

"Will you sit down," she said, and seated herself. "I expect you're tired, Uncle Robert, it's a long walk to and from Leominster."

"Yes, it is, and all I've had since my breakfast is a lump of bread and cheese and a pint of cider since, that's at the 'Tally-ho'."

"How many miles have we walked, Father?"

"Twelve miles me; you six miles," he said with a slight grin.

We sat talking for half an hour, but no refreshment appeared. I rose and said to my father, "Come Dad, let's go. I hope you have some food in the cottage, I'm starving."

Lil saw us to the door, the boys following, and said as we walked towards the gate, "I shall see you tonight, Elizabeth?"

"Yes, at about nine o'clock. Bye-bye for now," I replied.

Ten minutes later we arrived at Lower Woodlands and my main object after putting my case down and discarding my coat and hat, was to see about a meal. I was glad to see that my father had bought some furniture locally, having given up waiting for my mother to send it. I had not eaten since breakfast at eight o'clock except for the packet of biscuits and a glass of cider at the inn. Luckily Father had stocked up with quite a supply of food, and very soon we were sitting down to a substantial meal of eggs and bacon. There was of course no electricity or gas; lighting was provided by oil lamps and candles.

Afterwards we sat back to rest, the walk had been tiring on a hot day, my suitcase heavy.

"You never finished that story about Uncle Ted," I said.

"No," said my father. "Where were we? Oh yes. Well, your aunt decided to go into Leominster with him, wanted something special, I suppose. He didn't want her to go, said he'd do any shopping she wanted. No, she'd go herself, she said. Well, of course Ted never passed the 'Tally-ho', either going to market, or coming back, and the old horse got to know it. When Ted went in for a drink, he used to give the horse her nosebag and she had a feed out of it while he was inside. Well, this day the old mare pulled up as usual outside the pub, but of course as your aunt was with him, he didn't want to stay. He rattled the reins on her back, but she wouldn't go on. 'Edward' your aunt said, 'I see you have been making a regular habit of stopping here, and old Molly knows it.' The same thing happened coming back from the market but Ted didn't dare get out for a drink."

I was anxious to look the house over and perhaps to see something of the ground before going to my cousin's place for the night.

"Clear the table and leave everything and come down through the grounds, I have a surprise for you," said my father. We went out through the little gate on to the road. On the opposite side was a sizeable meadow, and a plot of ground my father said he would use to grow vegetables. Further down the road on the same side as the house were two large orchards, parted by a large field gate, and a wide cart track which led to a neighbour's field which had been planted with corn.

In the far orchard were two young calves, grazing peacefully on the bright green grass — Father said they were about sixteen weeks old, and in a few months they would fetch a good price in the market. "Don't go too near them, they're frisky when they are that age, and might kick you." They were two little Herefords, with white faces which they turned to gaze at us, then after a moment or two they resumed grazing. Little did I know the trouble they would cause me before they made that journey to the market. There were also two pigs in a sty near the house.

We returned to the house at last, and I was free to look round. The house and dairy were much as my father had said, but the rooms were small, and I realised that much of our own furniture would not have gone into it, especially as my father had already furnished the rooms from a local auction. There were a table and two chairs in the kitchen-cum-sitting room, as well as basic furniture upstairs, though there was no bed linen of any kind. The scullery door led out to the back of the house. Outside to the left was a large stone wheel, about thirty inches across and about eighteen inches high. My father explained it was a stone wheel used to crush apples for making cider. The previous owners had at some time made their own cider, he said, and the cider-mill was still in the barn. He showed me and explained that the deep stone trough which was built in a circle took the apples plus some water. The stone wheel was fixed to run inside this trough. There was a special harness so you could get a horse to pull it over the apples and break them into a pulp. Then when the apples were crushed they were placed in heavy cloth especially made for the purpose, and put into a press, where all the juice was squeezed out into a large tub. The juice was then barrelled and left until it was fit to drink.

We left the barn and went across the yard to look at the pigsty and cowshed. A large field gate opened on to the road.

It was dusk when we each set off to our respective abodes for the night.

3

That evening I met my cousin Paul for the first time. I had never met any of my father's relatives, though I had heard a lot about my Uncle Ted during my childhood. My father thought so highly of him that I had got the impression that he must be quite an exceptional man. Of my Aunt Lizzie and my cousins I had heard little.

Paul and Lil were sitting by the fire (as the evenings were still chilly) waiting for me. "The children are in bed long since," Lil said. Paul was a man of about forty, tall, thickset, with a heavy black moustache. He greeted me kindly and invited me to sit by the fire, and we talked quite a while about my life in Cardiff. Did I like it there? I told him I had been very happy there, and had been nurse to two little boys of whom I was very fond. "Oh well, if you like little boys, there's three here you can fuss over in your spare time. Your father said you'd have plenty of spare time and you'd be able to give Lil a hand."

I laughed and told him Father had so many plans that I could see myself kept very busy for quite a while. The garden was very overgrown and, as things should have been planted by now, so he said, I could see myself putting in a full-time job on that. The house badly needed attention: in every room the wallpaper was old and torn. The paintwork, particularly on the window frames was peeling.

To this neither replied. There was silence as Lil stared at me with a half-smile. Somehow I felt she was trying to see inside me. I felt uncomfortable.

On the table was a large white jug. Paul picked it up and poured out what I took to be cider. When he had half-emptied the glass he put it on the table and asked me if I would like some.

"No, thank you Paul, I don't think I'd sleep well on cider. I'd like to go to bed now, Lil," I said to her as she gazed into the fire. "I've got to be down at Woodlands to cook breakfast at eight in the morning, Boss's orders."

Paul chuckled. "Uncle Robert will be up early then, to get down there after a two-mile walk, by eight o'clock."

"Well, he won't be stopping at Uncle Ted's for breakfast. He said he would get up and come straight down. All the same I expect Uncle Ted will be up, he's got cows to milk, hasn't he?"

Paul said his father had two cows, but he couldn't see his father getting up before seven in the morning — he had no liking for early morning. With that, Lil stood up and took me to the bedroom I was to share with the oldest little boy, whose name, she said was Edward, after his grandad. (Roy was the second one and the baby was Malcolm.)

Although I was very tired, sleep did not come. I lay and thought of all that had happened that day, of the little boys I had left in Cardiff, of their mother who had always been so good to me, of Dr Armstrong, who had always had a kindly smile for me, and of Phyllis the housemaid. We had got on well together. On Easter Day Mrs Armstrong had put two parcels on the breakfast table, one for Phyllis, and one for me. When we opened them we found two lovely chocolate eggs, gaily wrapped in bright paper, and in pretty boxes. That had happened at both the Easters I had been there. I had treasured the boxes long after the eggs had been eaten. I had often looked in the shop windows and seen the display of Easter eggs, some with fluffy baby chicks, but I had never bought one, for it took practically all my wages to keep me reasonably dressed. Thirty shillings a month did not go far, even in those days of cheap clothing and food, and I had never felt that I could afford such an extravagance. So I had been thrilled with the presents. Yes, those two years had been the happiest of my life.

At last I fell asleep.

That April morning in 1918 when I began my new life with Father was bright and sunny. Birds whistled among the green leaves but half-grown and all the world seemed fair to me. As I walked down the road from Lil's, near to the left turning I saw an old whitewashed house with a thatched roof. Standing outside was a man of about seventy, enjoying the sunshine. As I approached he pulled a large red and white handkerchief from his pocket and blew his nose noisily into it. He seemed in no way embarrassed, having thus drawn attention to himself, and called a cheerful "Good morning to you, Miss". I replied, but kept walking.

"Be you the young woman that be acoming to live at Woodlands?"

I stopped and replied, "Yes. Mr Walker is my father."

The door behind him opened and an old lady stepped out. She was short and plump with rosy cheeks and twinkling blue eyes, and wore a large apron that went almost entirely round her. Her hair, parted in the middle, shining like silver, was pulled tightly to the back of her head. She smiled and said, "You're going to live at Woodlands, I heard you tell my husband, I hope you will like it. We are not your nearest neighbours but anyway we are only five minutes away from you." I said I would see her again, but that I must be going as my father would be waiting for me. I moved off a few steps, then stopped, as the old man, raising his voice a little called, "Be you Welsh?"

"Yes," I said.

He considered a minute then said, "Pity, I don't like Welsh people, hm. Pity."

"What's your name?" I said to him.

"Benson, William Benson," he replied as once more he applied his handkerchief to his nose, and blew vigorously.

"That's a pity, Mr Benson, but I expect I'll survive," I said as I walked on.

I reached the cottage gate just as my father arrived. We walked up the cobble-stoned path and as we entered the door my father said, "What did you think of Paul?"

"Well, I can't say. We only talked a bit. Lil was there, but she hardly spoke. She kept staring at me as though she was weighing me up. I don't like people who stare so."

"Lil doesn't have much to talk about I'm thinking. She's there day in day out, while Paul is out doing the farm work. Often he takes his food and cider out to the fields and doesn't come back till milking time."

"Paul says you've promised I should go up and help them, but I told him it seemed to me there was plenty to do here, what with the garden and doing up the house."

"Oh, yes, yes," my father said testily, "that's so. Still, I shall have to let you go and help her, as she is not taking anything for your sleeping there. I think you could help her when there's a chance, not for a while of course, we shall be busy here."

When breakfast was over, we started work on the garden clearing weeds and rubbish. We broke off for a lunch of bread and cheese and cider, but at the end of the day we seemed to have made little progress as there was so much to remove before we could start digging.

That evening before my father went up to my uncle's we fed the pigs and brought the two calves down from the orchard to the cowshed, as it was still too cold at night for them to be out. I drove them down on to the road, and as I had left the big gate that led into the yard open, they turned into the yard, all by themselves. "I felt I could have managed the job myself," I told my father.

Next morning there was a letter from Mother. Over breakfast my father read it out loud to me. My mother had not been well. She would not be coming, as she felt she would not be happy, but she was sending down the bed linen. About this my father said little. But I was pleased that my mother was at least sending the bed linen. I hoped she would remember soon to send some curtains. But I was disappointed that she was not coming too — I could have gone to work for myself again.

We had not been digging long in the garden when I heard slow footsteps coming down the road. An old man of about eighty was walking on two walking sticks.

My father whispered, "The tenant of Upper Woodlands."

He opened the gate, walked up the path, and came into

the garden. He was tall and very thin, with a red face and piercing blue eyes that looked at you from under bushy eyebrows. His jacket was heavily patched, and he wore corduroy trousers. A cloth cap was tightly pulled down on to his head but I was amused to see he had a piece of material sewn into the back of his cap, which hung down over his coat collar. There was a large wart on the side of his nose.

"I have seen Mr Walker before, my dear, I was talking to him a few days ago, and I'm making a guess that you must be his daughter. How are you? My name is Pressley, John Pressley."

"Oh, how do you do, Mr Pressley. Yes, I'm Elizabeth Walker."

"Got a good old job on there haven't you? Well, of course the old people that lived here got beyond it and of course the place has been idle six months." As he spoke he dug the bottoms of his walking sticks into the ground and settled his behind on the handles. "A garden soon gets out of shape when it's been left so long. No doubt about it at all." My father took no notice, but went on with his work, and I dared not stop either.

"There's a turning just a few yards up the road, about a hundred yards or so, you know, that cart track that goes between my father's meadow and another field. Are there any cottages down there? I heard some children playing down there," I said.

"Yes, there are. There be two houses down there. One is where Mrs Jones lives and her's got four kids, three boys and a girl. Her man works at Bowes Farm, and the house her lives in belongs to Bowes Farm. The other cottage belongs to two sisters — old maids they be, and Mr Davies of Bowes Farm wants to buy the cottage as they live in but they won't sell," said Mr Pressley, as he settled down more comfortably on his walking sticks.

I considered this a moment as I beat a clod of earth and grass with the spade to loosen the soil. At least there were neighbours quite close.

24

Father interrupted my thoughts. "You'd best go in and get the dinner on the way, I'll carry on here."

Mr Pressley got little encouragement to stay any longer. Father was not inclined to be friendly, and presently I heard Mr Pressley walking down the path.

4

"Now look here," my father said as he sat down to his dinner. "I don't want you getting too chatty with that old fool, or he'll hang round here too often to please me. He's got nothing else to do and we have and, as for neighbours, you don't want to bother about them either. Neighbours are no good to you, always interfering in your affairs and, besides that, Mrs Jones is no good to you. So don't let me see you talking to her. Keep to yourself."

"How do you know they're not nice people, Father. Have you spoken to them?"

"No, I haven't and I don't want to. Not to Jones or his wife, but their kids were climbing on the orchard gate and I had to go and tell them to get off."

No more was said and dinner was eaten in silence. I had been brought up very much on my own as a child and not allowed to play with children in the street in Abercynon, at least not when my father was at home and that was nearly every evening after five-thirty when he returned from the coal mine. On odd occasions he would go to visit his younger brother who lived about twenty minutes' walk away; otherwise he worked at home in the garden or sat indoors and read the evening paper. He never approved of my mother talking to the neighbours, and it was Father's boast that although he had lived in the same house for twenty-five years he had never spoken to the neighbours except to pass the time of day. I understood then why my mother had of late sought out her own friends and had declined to come and live in the country. "I am not going to be buried alive amongst your relations in the country," she had told him. She knew my father and his ways. In Cardiff, in the home I shared with the Armstrongs I had found friendship and happiness, but now I realised the lonely days of my childhood were to be relived at Woodlands with my father.

But the day brightened up with the arrival of my trunk by carrier, and that evening after Father had gone to Uncle Ted's and Aunt Lizzie's, I spared a few minutes before I left for Lil's house to unpack and hang some of my clothes in a built-in cupboard, that would serve as wardrobe and boxroom.

Next morning was wet and as I walked down the road to the cottage I wondered if Father would bother to come down, but I was surprised to find he had arrived before me and was lighting the fire. Soon the kettle was placed on the sway, a hooked iron chain that hung over the fire. We had an old apple tree sawn up in the yard so that we could use those logs for burning, and the coal man, I was told, would call once every two weeks.

"Didn't think you would have come down, seeing it was so wet, Dad," I said.

"Well, I thought maybe it'll brighten up by and by; anyway your aunt wants me to take you up to see her tomorrow. We can't dig on a Sunday, so I said you should go up. If I meet you in the village instead of coming down here, it would save me walking down here for you."

This was agreed on, after Father had explained that I couldn't lose myself on the way to the village as it was a straight road to the church and then, round the corner, were the village shop, the butcher's and the only public house. He would meet me at the inn, at ten o'clock. All morning the rain teemed down and we sat by the fire. After dinner, it stopped, but it was impossible to work in the garden, so when I had washed up the dishes I sat by the fire again. There was nothing to do.

"Do you think they bring the daily papers down here, Father?"

"No, I shouldn't think so, your uncle gets one only on Sunday. Perhaps we'll be able to have one down here on Sundays too. We'll try and find out."

I tried to visualise the days ahead with no newspaper. It was almost impossible to believe that a war was going on, in this isolated spot.

"It will seem queer not to have a newspaper every day won't it? I mean, we've always been used to one every day," I said.

"No," said Father. "Not to me, and I think, too, the world would be far better off without so many papers. There would be less feeling between countries than there is if it wasn't for the newspapers always ready to publish what some misguided politician spouts about. Newspapers abroad get those statements and by the time the foreign papers publish it, it's often quite a distorted version of what's said."

I agreed this might be so and after a while Father decided that as there was little he could do he might just as well go up to Headlands Farm to Uncle Ted. "You may as well go up to Lil's," he said. "Maybe you could give her a hand at something."

"What about the cattle, Father? You won't put them in the cowshed this early?"

Father pondered a minute, "Hm, yes, there's them — too early to put them in."

I offered to come down later before it was dark, and get the calves in. Later I walked slowly up the road towards Benson's old cottage — some two hundred yards from Woodlands. I found a stretch of water across the road and as I looked beyond it to where I should have to go to get to Lil's farm I saw a torrent rushing down to the water already blocking my path. Standing there was not going to help matters as the water was getting deeper. It was spreading over the road and on to the green verge, so there was no way of walking round it.

I stepped into it and in a moment I found it was up to my knees. I had pulled my skirts up round me and on I went. At last I was on drier ground but I continued to hold my skirts up, not to get them wet, round my wet stockings. I took my boots off, poured the water out and put them on again. Eventually I reached the farm. Lil was sitting in the kitchen, the children playing round the empty fireplace on the hearth rug.

"You're back early," she said.

"Yes, Father couldn't get on with the garden. There was nothing he could do. I couldn't get on with house cleaning. I could have scrubbed the floors I suppose, but there's no pail in the house, so I decided I'd come on up here. Thought I could do something for you. As I came along the road I found the rain had collected. I suppose there's no drain to take the water away but it's just like a big pond by old Benson's place, and now look at me, soaked to my knees. Could you lend me a towel to wipe my legs? I shall have to get my stockings off and go barelegged, that's all, and barefoot too by the look of it, my boots are saturated."

Lil got up, and opening the dairy door, reached round it for a towel and handed it to me.

"I can find you a pair of slippers, they may be too big, but they're better than putting those wet boots on." I thanked Lil and very soon I felt more comfortable. The boys were playing noisily with some bricks, building them up as high as they could, then knocking them down amid shouts and laughter.

"Steady up, Ted, it's Roy's turn to knock them down. Take it in turns now, you can't do it all the time." Roy knocked the bricks down and soon they were scrambling to build them up again.

"Do they find plenty to amuse them round here? I mean are there children round here for them to play with?"

"Well, not really. Ted and Roy go to school. Malcolm won't be so long before he goes, but he finds it lonesome by himself while they're away. Otherwise they amuse each other and are quite happy. I must light the fire, I haven't bothered to keep it in, I didn't feel it was cold, but now I must get some hot water — I have dinner dishes to wash and I must feed the poultry."

"I'll wash the dishes for you Lil, if you want to go and feed the poultry. I'll light the fire too — is this the wood to light it?" I pointed to a large pan by the side of the fire which had wood from the hedges. "Oh yes, that will start it and Ted will show you where to get some thicker wood once it's lit. It's in the shed outside on the left."

"I expect you use a lot of wood, I mean there must be plenty round here?"

"Oh yes, lots. Paul finds an old apple tree that is past bearing and down it comes, and of course there's always wood from the hedges." As Lil said this she put on an old overcoat (it was raining again), and an old trilby hat.

"It's awful," she said, jamming the hat firmly on to her head, "but it keeps the rain out same as my old coat. Not worth tuppence. Still it keeps me dry when it's wet, and warm when it's cold. I'll be off now. Oh, yes, hang the kettle on that hook over the fire."

With that Lil was gone. The fire burned well and with Ted as guide I found the woodshed and carried an armful of small logs into the house.

By the time Lil was back the kettle had boiled, the dishes were washed, the kettle refilled and put on again. The children chatted a lot about school. When I asked them, did they like school? Did they have to walk to school? They replied that Daddy took them in the horse and trap when it was wet, otherwise they walked. It was quite a long walk — over a mile. Sometimes they took a short cut through the fields.

Presently Lil came back bearing a bucket nearly a third full with eggs.

"Have you many chickens, Lil?"

"Well," she said, taking the bucket into the dairy, "I have two hundred and fifty layers, and a hundred new ones about three months old. They are to replace some of the older ones, of course this lot of eggs I've brought in now is a third collection. Won't be any more today I don't expect." She took her coat and hat off and hung them behind the door.

"Do you look after the poultry altogether, or does Paul help you, or you help him?" I said, laughing.

"Oh no, he doesn't touch the poultry side. They are mine, and so my job. The poultry is mine, the profits mine, I pay for their food, I buy wheat off Paul at threshing time. You see, we grow wheat and oats ourselves, then I pay him market price for whatever I want. Paul has given me one field to keep them on."

"That sounds nice to me, Lil. You have your own pocket money, or clothes money. I'd like my father to let me do that; otherwise I can see my clothes wearing out and no money to replace them, unless of course he will give me some money

30

now and then. My boots won't be much good after this wetting and I've got to go down through that water again to get those calves in — oh dear, and back through it again to get up here. They'll be about finished. I still have my wages from my job, that's thirty shillings. I shall have to spend a pound on boots now, but these would have done me a while if it wasn't for this soaking," I said, going to the door to look at the rain as it teemed down. "You were back in time to dodge this shower, Lil. Paul is very good to let you keep the income from the poultry, isn't he?"

"Well no, not really, because it's the usual way, round here at least. The farmer's wife has the poultry like me. The cows, now, we have nine cows, pay the house expenses. I make butter from the cream, that goes to my grocer, the butter I mean. Then each week my groceries are paid for by the money I would get for the butter and I draw whatever cash is over. That pays for the coal, what bit I buy, and also pays for the children's clothes. I pay for my own. Paul has the pigs. When he sells some, the cash goes to his bank account. He pays the rent. If he sells young eight-week-old piglets, that goes to him. If he buys he has the cash and I never ask him what he has, he never asks me what I have — so you see, we each have our own banking account, such as it is. That is the general way, my sisters are farmers' wives, my brothers' wives do the same and so does Gran."

I was surprised and pleased to find Lil so talkative. I had thought her so reserved.

"I'm going up to see Aunt Lizzie and Uncle Ted tomorrow, Lil. Father told me this morning that he had been told to take me up. Anyway it's Sunday and we could not work in the garden. I am to meet him in the village."

I looked at the clock and saw it was nearly teatime.

"If you'd like to stay for tea, you can. There will be plenty of time and you could go later to see to the cattle. Maybe the water will have gone down some, if not all. I don't think it will be all gone though. After a rain like we have had it's sometimes there a couple of days," Lil said, putting the kettle on again. "This has already boiled, so it won't take long to get boiled again."

When tea was over I washed up and it occurred to me I had not seen Paul. I asked Lil why he had not been home to tea. "He is up at Headlands with his father. He should have been home before this, but hasn't hurried himself I suppose, seeing he could not do much outside today. But there's the pigs to feed and the cows to fetch in to dry a bit before milking, so he should be here soon."

I decided I would go off down to Woodlands and get the calves into the shed. My boots were now a bit drier, but I thought it best to leave my stockings off as they were still very wet.

I found that in the time I had been at Lil's the lake on the road had increased. I waded through and after pouring the water out of my boots put them on and ran down to the yard. I opened the field gate and went down to the field and called the cattle. They came quite easily out of the field, up the road, and into the cowhouse. I was very glad they had been so little trouble. Very soon they were happily eating hay, while I rubbed their backs with straw.

The house was cold and uninviting. I found my only pair of shoes and wrapped them up to take back with me to Lil's farm. I was glad to leave and pleased to get back to the warmth of Lil's fire.

5

On Sunday the sun shone, the sky was blue and I was happy to feel I was going out for the day. After I had returned to Woodlands I made my way for the first time towards Dilwyn village. There were a number of cottages on each side of the road and a tin chapel. The village was quite sizeable, with old houses with white walls and black beams and small windows like eyes looking on to the road. Father met me at the inn and soon we were at Headlands Farm.

My aunt and uncle were at the door to meet us. "We guessed you were on the way, the old dog hears footfalls long before anyone is in sight," said Aunt Lizzie. She was a small, slim woman of over sixty with cheeks like rosy apples, grey sparkling eyes and white shining hair pulled back tightly into a small bun. In the collar of her black dress she wore a cameo brooch. I took an instant liking to Aunt Lizzie. After I had greeted her, I turned to Uncle Ted and said, "How do you do, Uncle, I've heard such a lot about you from my father."

"I'm pleased to see you too. Come now, wench, give your uncle a kiss," he said, grabbing my arm. He was tall, like my father, and about four years older than him. White-haired, that showed fairly long beneath his old trilby hat. He wore breeches and leggings and strong hob-nailed boots.

"Well, how did you like your walk? Those shoes", he said, looking at them, "were never meant for country walks, they'm got stilts, not heels. How do you manage to walk on them?" (As my boots were still wet, I had put on my best shoes.)

"Yes, ridiculous," said Father before I could answer. "If the Almighty meant us to walk on high heels then he'd have made us that way. He wouldn't have meant us to have imitations. Simply vanity, that's what it is, and vanity is sinful."

My face went crimson under the stare of the two men. Aunt relieved the embarrassment by saying, "Well now, let's go in, no point in standing out here. Let's go into the kitchen and sit down, Edward. I expect Robert would like some cider and you too, Elizabeth, would you like some, my dear?"

Uncle Ted disappeared with a large white jug and very soon returned with it full of golden cider. Glasses were produced and very soon we were sitting down enjoying the lovely cool drink.

"Do you make much cider, Uncle?" I said.

"Oh yes, quite a lot, quite a lot. Have to, we're all of us used to cider-drinking round these parts. I allus reckon to keep an 'ogshead for haymaking time and make two 'ogshead for ordinary times," said Uncle as he put his glass on the table.

"Ogshead — what's an ogshead?" I said.

"An 'ogshead is a barrel that holds a hundred gallons, my dear, and your uncle makes much more than he ought to, but he suffers with a great thirst, but he's never thirsty enough ever to drink water. The only time he ever drinks water is when the water is used to make tea," said Aunt Lizzie laughing.

"You know," said Uncle as he poured another glass of cider for Father and himself, "your aunt should have married a parson, or a parson's son, someone who objects to anything stronger than tea — not a man like me, who was weaned on cider when a babby."

My father changed the subject. "I'll go up and change my clothes, Ted, and we'll go and see the pigs, while Elizabeth gives Lizzie a hand to get dinner."

Very soon they were outside and my aunt and myself settled down to chat for a few moments.

"I hope, my dear, you will settle down with your father. I know it's a different life to what you have been used to, but he needs someone to look after him. Do you think your mother will come down here eventually?"

"I don't know, Aunt, I'm sure. But I would like to feel that she would come. I am not used to the country although I don't dislike it now. I shall always be wanting to go back to work and earn money. I shall have to buy new boots very soon, I ruined mine yesterday."

"How? What happened?"

I explained about the water blocking the road on my way to Lil's house and that I had had to go through it twice afterwards when I had had to come down to put the cattle in and that although the day was fine now, the water, although it had lessened in quantity from the previous night, was still out on the road. It was deep enough to soak my shoes, when I had come down to the cottage that morning.

We talked about lots of things as we prepared dinner and I liked my aunt very much. After a long while and dinner nearly ready, it occurred to us that we had not seen either of the two men for over an hour!

I was told to look for them.

"Don't go any further than the barn. I expect you'll find them in there," said Aunt.

As she had predicted, they were in the barn sitting on the straw each with a glass in his hand.

"I have just been making a deal with your uncle," said Father. "I am going to buy five eight-week-old pigs from him, and we will bring them down to our place in the morning. We'll show you them after dinner." With that he got up off the straw.

"Dinner is ready, and Aunt is dishing up, so I have been sent to fetch you," I said.

"Come on then, Robert. When the old girl says dinner is ready, there's trouble if the call isn't answered," said Uncle as he rose slowly from the straw and started for the door. He turned round and looked behind him. "I thought the jug was out here. Go and get it, wench, we will have some cider with our dinner." I was soon back with the jug. Uncle filled it and we trooped into the house.

We were soon enjoying a good dinner — a joint of beef, roast potatoes and freshly-cooked vegetables, all done on an old-fashioned coal-grate with two large ovens one each side of the fire. My aunt told me that she baked all the bread they used, and that Lil did the same. "You see, we have to. Bread is not delivered so far out of the village, the houses are too scattered."

We went on chatting for quite a while, my uncle producing stories about local goings-on, then the men disappeared. They were probably, said Aunt, having a look round the grounds, or were in the barn, along with the cider.

We had tidied up and Aunt had put on her Sunday dress, ready for going to chapel. Some time later the two men returned.

"Well," said Father, "we were talking about your getting back home, weren't we, Ted? I thought perhaps you could go home alone, you couldn't lose your way to the village. I'll come down in the morning about nine. I'll help Ted get his work done, then we will bring the pigs down. He has a net to put over them, once we have them up in the trap. Do you think you could go home alone?"

I found my way home to Woodlands and changed my clothes and had supper before going to get the two heifers into the cowshed. I meant to get to Paul's farm before dusk. I went into the small meadow where the cattle were lying but found one of the heifers could not stand despite all my efforts. I watched her with dismay. She seemed to be trembling. I tried again and again to get her to rise on to her feet, but it was no good. Then I thought of the neighbours, the Joneses or the two spinster ladies. Dare I ask them for assistance?

I came out of the meadow and turned down the lane, to find the Jones's house. It was just about a hundred yards down the lane as Mr Pressley had said. There was a large garden in front and two of the children were playing there. I went up to the door and knocked. It was opened by a short plump woman, who I guessed would be Mrs Jones.

I explained that my father had taken over Woodlands and I had hoped to have come to have introduced myself to her before this, but that Father and I had been very busy on the garden for days and that now I had come, I had come hoping for some help. With that, Mr Jones came to the door. He was elderly and almost bald.

"What's the matter, my dear?" he said as he put his cap on. I explained what had happened, and asked if he could come and look and tell me what to do? He came with me to the meadow and stood watching the heifer a while.

"Her's got a chill, that's what's the matter with her — see, how she's trembling? Aye, it's a chill for sure. We'll get her up somehow. Can't leave her here, her's got to get in the cowshed."

With much difficulty we made her get up off the ground and very slowly we walked the two heifers back to the cowshed, where the sick one immediately lay down on the straw. The other tucked into the hay and mangolds my father had left for them.

"Well," said Mr Jones as he stood looking at the sick animal. "You'm best go and tell your Dad, you see, she needs a drench."

"What's a drench, Mr Jones?"

"Well," said Mr Jones, as he scratched his head at the back. "A drench is a dose of medicine, like you'd take a pill or a dose yourself if so be you had a cold or a chill. Mind you, I could give her a drench, and t'would save you a going to fetch your Dad, but I don't know him and he would p'raps rather I didn't, so my gell the best advice I can give you is to fetch him quick. Where is he?"

"Staying with my Uncle Ted up at Headlands," I replied.

"Ah yes, I knows him, Ted Walker, yes, went to school with him, or at least same time as him, he's a bit older than me. He was born in Ludlow, same as me."

I thanked Mr Jones for his help and went into the house to get my hat and coat. The time was past eight-thirty. The walk to my Uncle's would take me about forty-five minutes at least and it would be dark before I got to the farm.

By the time I reached the village it was quite dark. The only light came from behind drawn curtains. The village inn was bright and noisy as I passed. I hurried on, fearful of the dark lonely road, a road still strange to me. I must look out for the turning, I told myself, or goodness knows where I should end up. After I had gone about half a mile out of the village as I walked along the road, two lights but faintly shone over the top of the low hedge. My heart fluttered with fright and for a moment I stood still.

I decided I must go on, whatever I could see would become clearer to me as I advanced. As I drew nearer I made out the dark shape of a head, then I saw the thing that frightened me was none other than a cow which was merely standing close to the hedge.

At last I reached the farm. As I unlatched the cart gate the dog began to bark. I remembered his kennel was just outside the house and it was possible he was fastened, but, as I told myself I would soon know if he was allowed loose, he would be around my heels in a moment.

I stood still and listened. The bark came from the direction of the house and I realised he was fastened. In a moment or two the upstairs window opened and a head poked out.

"Who's there?" That was Uncle Ted's voice.

"Uncle, it's Elizabeth, I have come after Father. One of the young cattle is ill and he had better come down to see what is to be done for it."

Father must have heard me because I heard him call, "All right, Ted, don't bother to go down, I'll be down in five minutes. Tell the dog to lay down, he'll awake the neighbourhood."

Uncle gave a grunt, his head was withdrawn and I heard the click of the window as it was fastened. Very soon Father joined me. I shivered. I had not noticed the night had turned quite cold but as I stood waiting for him I was glad I had my coat on and pulled the collar closely round my neck. I told him I had had to seek help from the neighbour, Mr Jones. Mr Jones had said that the animal had got a chill and that it needed a drench.

"I have no drench at the house so that means we must either go back to your uncle for some or go to Beacon Farm to Paul," he said. I told him it would be better to go to Paul, that they must be wondering what had happened to me.

"They must have waited up for me and when I was so late have gone to bed," I said.

"It must be about midnight now," said Father, "or not far off. I don't like going up to disturb them this time of night, but there's nothing else for it, I suppose." So we made for Beacon Farm before going to Woodlands.

Paul's old sheepdog had a kennel outside the back door, but I was used to him and was able to quieten him when he started to bark.

Their bedroom lay to the front of the house and after we had knocked loudly on the door several times, the door was opened by my disgruntled cousin.

We apologised and told him what had happened. Father asked him if he had anything suitable to use as a drench and he produced a bottle from the cupboard.

"That should have hot water to use it properly. Take the bottle and use about two tablespoonfuls to about a cup of water. I should give her another dose in the morning, if I were you."

I told my cousin I would not come back again that night but would sit in the cottage till breakfast time but I would be up as usual the following evening.

"It will be daylight soon, anyway," he said. "Gets light now about four o'clock. You had better take this too." Out of the cupboard he produced a hollow cowhorn. "Put the narrow end in the heifer's mouth, and pour the liquid into the wide end. Make sure she swallows it, then cover her with straw, and leave her to sweat it out. You'll most likely find her on her feet in the morning, but you'd best keep them both in for a few days."

We set off for our own cottage. I remembered I had hidden the key under a stone outside the house. Soon were indoors, and it was the work of a few minutes to light the fire and lower the kettle down onto the flames, and soon it was boiling. While my father was making the drench, I made a pot of tea and covered it with a towel, in the hope that it might still be hot when we had finished.

My father stood astride the animal and pulled back her head, opening her mouth. "Now!" he said. I inserted the horn and poured the drench in. Thankfully it went down.

Afterwards we didn't talk much, we were too tired. Father put some more wood on the fire; we had some hot tea and settled on the chairs to sleep the three hours left of the night.

6

In the morning, although the heifer could not stand, she looked brighter and had stopped trembling.

While we ate breakfast my father decided we should go out into the garden until eight o'clock when he would return the drench to Paul and then go to Uncle Ted, to get the pigs into the trap. I had to go to the village to get provisions and tobacco for my father when the shops opened at about nine. Father insisted that I must be back by the time the pigs were settled into the shed.

"We must get on with the garden. In the three days we have been at it we've not made much headway, but if the weather holds dry for the next four days this garden should be finished. Then we must get on with the one on the other side of the road."

I set off for the village. Now I had time to look around me. There were several whitewashed cottages, with thatched roofs, their small windows shining like diamonds in the bright sunlight, with large front gardens all planted out, every one with a border of flowers each side of the path leading to the front door. Some cottages were more modern, built of brick and tile as was the Hollands' farm where we collected our milk each day; then, the little bridge that crossed the stream, and the Catholic church, and then the big farm at the bottom of the village. As I neared the farm I could hear guinea fowl. 'Go back, go back,' they seemed to say. Next were three little cottages in a row with just one single gateway between them, and a very large garden that must have been common to the three; then the lovely old church, with its ancient tombstones. There were two entrances to the church from the crossroads. The main entrance had a wide path leading up to the porch. I walked through the open gates. On either side were tomb-stones and one was dated 1670. The pathway swept round to the back of the church to a courtyard. I guessed that people who came by horse and carriage or traps could leave them there. I would have liked to have gone into the church but mindful of the fact that Father would be waiting for me to make another meal, I decided to wait till another day.

At the village shop there were several customers before me so I had to wait a while to be served. Besides grocery there were boots and shoes, hanging by their laces from a rope line that stretched the length of the room. Along another rope line was wearing apparel of various kinds. There was meal for pigs and poultry, and in a sack on the floor was (so the label attached said) 'Best Dairy Feed Nuts' for cows. On a shelf I saw medicines for horses and cattle and another shelf held medicines and ointments for the family. Partitioned off was a small space used as a post office. I marvelled that they could put their hand on request amongst such a variety, and said so to the shopkeeper when it was at last my turn to be served.

"It's being used to it, my gell, it is. We've been here ten years now, so I suppose we are about used to it now. Took a bit of getting used to at first, though, I can tell you," said the man behind the counter whilst a plump woman, whom I guessed must be his wife, laughed and wobbled all over. I said I thought his speech sounded of a Welsh accent.

"Yes, my gell, and so does yours. We came here from the Rhondda Valley, worked in the pits I did, until we came here, ten years ago. I had to give up my job as the result of an accident in the mine. There was a big explosion underground and a lot were killed. Some of us were trapped in one place for three days in the dark. Well, we were rescued; we were lucky at least we came out alive; others were not so lucky. I was hurt, and when I got better I made up my mind that I had finished with the coal mines for good. There were several little lads of fourteen who had not long left school down there, and they never came up again and they were never found. Buried by a huge fall of coal. But what part do you come from?" said the man as he leaned on the counter.

"Abercynon," I said.

"Oh yes, I know it well, so does the wife, don't you, Margett?"

"Yes, we do," replied Margett. "I know some people there still as a matter of fact."

The conversation was halted by more arrivals at the shop so I purchased my groceries. But I could only get my father a small amount of tobacco as supplies to the village were erratic, and the shopkeeper said that he preferred to ration it to his customers. I decided next time I came I would buy a pair of strong boots —they would cost me a pound.

I hurried off down the road. I had been longer than I had intended and when I got home I saw Uncle's trap outside. My father and Uncle Ted were both sitting by the empty fireplace. Father had let the fire go out, but they did not seem to mind. Each had a glass of cider in his hand.

I saw that the postman had called and that there was a letter from my mother.

I relit the fire and put the kettle over it to make a cup of tea, and after setting the dishes I went out to the yard.

The piglets were round and white, about the size of small puppies. They had left their mother only that morning but when Father poured some meal and water into the long trough in the pig run they guzzled it down greedily.

"When are you coming up to our place again?" said Uncle Ted.

"One of these days, Uncle, when I can, but there seems to be a lot to do here — at least until the gardens are dug and planted. But as soon as I can I'll be up to see Aunt again," I said as I poured the tea.

"Well, I'll be glad of a bit of help from you any time you have spare time," Uncle said as he drank his tea noisily.

"Help, Uncle — in which way?"

"Well, we shall have hay-making, fruit-picking and potato-picking and when we've cut the corn, your father's promised me a couple of days — we'll be glad to have you come up to help — there's tying up the wheat and barley, so you'll not be short of a job, I can find you one."

"Does Aunt help outside, Uncle?"

"Well, no. Her's got the poultry to see to — then there's the milking pails and pans to wash night and morning, milk to separate, butter to make once a week, so her hasn't much time for outside work I'm afraid. Then, of course, house and cooking to do too."

I let the matter pass. I had no intention of making myself a farmhand for Uncle Ted but when he had departed Father brought the matter up as we had a second breakfast.

"Well, of course, it won't hurt you to give your Uncle a hand an odd day now and then. He's got a lot to do and I expect we could arrange it when things are straightened up a bit, don't you think?"

"No, Father, I don't think. You say when things are straightened out, you said the other day you must get some work on one of the farms. Well, don't you think I shall have enough to do here — there'll be the cattle and the pigs for me to see to? You said you intended getting some broody hens to put eggs under, to get some chicks. I'll have that to see to — there'll be the housework and washing. You will have your own hay-making and fruit-picking to do and I shall be able to help you with that, but I think between it all I shall have plenty to do here."

Father was silent for a few moments then said, "We shall see by and by, no need to bother for the time being."

"Have you forgotten that you have promised Lil I shall help her? Well, as I am sleeping up there it seems the only way to pay her, and I have promised to go up to help her make the butter every Thursday morning for two hours. Apart from that I'm sure I am not going to find any time to help anyone else." So saying I rose from the table and began clearing dishes and food away. I had made up my mind Father must clear his obligations to Uncle Ted without any assistance from me.

I glanced on the mantelpiece and remembered Mother's letter was still unread.

"I had forgotten in the excitement of the pigs coming and Uncle Ted being here, there's a letter from Mother. Read it — see what she says."

44

Father read the letter. "She is sending the bed linen today, Tuesday, by rail, and we must make arrangements to collect it from the station, hm, now what's to be done? Perhaps your uncle will know who I can get to haul it. I suppose we shall have a notice from the railway?" said Father. I said I thought so, but wanted to know what other news Mother gave. Father said that Mother had said nothing about coming down to Woodlands — in fact, she had got a job working in a munitions factory and quite able to keep herself. She was happy. She was going to live in Coventry. Country life would not suit her, she said.

The next two days were spent working in the garden but my father went to a local auction and bought some more furniture and some curtains and the bed linen arrived at the station. Mr Williams, the carrier, brought it from the station. I was allowed some time off from the gardening to get the house straight. I began laying linoleum down on the pine floor upstairs. I had claimed the bedroom furthest away from the stairs. It had a door I could shut. I had told Father I did not fancy sleeping in a room that led directly off the top step of the stairs.

Downstairs, I put all the chairs outside and set to to scrub the floor which was of stone flags. It was cold. I would have to prevail on Father to let me buy at least one coconut mat to put in front of the fire, but I thought I would wait a few days before mentioning it. When the floor was dry I arranged the chairs, and put out the blue and white crockery Father had bought on the dresser shelves. Suddenly I felt so happy — it looked like a home, and I would not have to walk to Lil's every night any more. At eleven my father came in and we had some bait — bread and cheese and cider — and then we were out in the garden again, planting until late afternoon when I was allowed in to cook the dinner. At nine o'clock that night we were both tired out but everything was in place. Father said he was glad he no longer had to walk two miles to Uncle Ted's farm. He said he had arranged to work several full days for Uncle in payment for being able to sleep at his house.

7

One evening after we had finished dinner, Father suggested we took a walk up to see Paul. The children were already in bed when we arrived, and we sat round the fire and talked. Lil said nothing though; it was like my father had said — she had spent nearly all her life in that farmhouse, leaving it seldom, except occasionally to go into Leominster on a market day. So I suppose to Lil there wasn't much to talk about, except the farm, pigs, chickens, children.

It was dusk when we left and dark by the time we got home. Father took the large old-fashioned key from his pocket and inserted it into the keyhole. The door would not open. We tried the door again and again. It wouldn't budge. "This is ridiculous," my father said. "The door locked quite easily when I fastened it coming out."

We stood and stared at each other. "What do we do now?"

The door at the front of the house had been locked from inside and the key was still in the lock. The two lower windows which were small were fastened also. Already it was about ten-thirty. We both sat down on the stone wheel outside the back door. From time to time my father would get up and try the door — he must have tried it at least a dozen times. We were well and truly locked out. The dairy window had an iron grill fixed on the inside, so there was no hope of entering that way. The other window was in the scullery and had not been opened for years. We must have sat outside on the stone wheel for all of six hours. It grew light again. My father looked at his watch. It was five-thirty.

"We must do something," I said. "We have to get in

somehow." In exasperation, I stood up and tried to turn the key in the lock again. To my surprise, the key turned and the door opened as easily as it had done many times before.

The days passed and after the house had been arranged to my liking I spent all the time I could helping Father get both gardens dug and planted, and very soon little green shoots came out of the ground and we were pleased that results were fast growing from our labour. The apple blossom was beautiful, the trees, all planted in rows from bottom to top of the orchard, were a blaze of colour, some blossom white, some pink. The pear trees too showed fine promise. The grass was getting long and lush in the lower orchard and meadow. This we were to let grow for the hay. The little heifer was now quite better and went out with the other one into the meadow.

My father was pleased with the progress of the five piglets and the two older ones were growing well. One of them when a bit bigger would be killed for home use, and the other whom we named Sally would soon be put to the boar. Father had ordered a couple of broody hens from Aunt Lizzie and one morning a card arrived by post asking Father to collect them. He decided to go up early next morning and spent a full day helping Uncle. That was when I decided to do the washing. I got the copper filled with water from the spout — several buckets full — and made a wood fire. Goodness knows when the copper had been used last, but I suppose it was very damp in the chimney for the smoke, instead of going up it, billowed into the scullery — and I had to stick the doors wide open and go out into the yard to breathe. But after a while it did clear, and I was able to put some water in my tub. The water was hard. I put handfuls of soda into it to soften it and lowered the sheets and towels in. I had to handwash because I had not yet bought a washing board. I had never in my life done a week's washing. In my job with the Armstrongs I was able to put all my washing, my uniform caps and aprons, into the laundry that was collected each Monday and brought back beautifully done on Fridays.

I rubbed the sheets and pillowcases and towels by hand and

the strong soda in the water made my hands smart. When it came to my father's Welsh flannel shirts that my mother had always made for him, their coarseness made my hands worse and I vowed I would go to the village the very next day and buy both the boots and a washing board out of my last ten shillings for three shillings and eleven pence (which I did). But now I had to get this lot finished: rinsed, squeezed by hand as best I could, and spread out on the hedges to dry. It seemed that everyone round there dried their washing that way. Once that was done, I cleaned up the scullery, having emptied out the water from the copper and dried it out. I cleaned the wood ash out of the grate and under it, after which I felt I had done the hardest day's work in all my life.

I had just got back from the village the next morning when Mr Pressley called to see me. He had been going for a walk but when he saw me getting water from the spout he decided to go no further.

"I must see your wife one of these days, Mr Pressley," I said, as I walked towards the gate where he was standing.

"Oh, Ada?" he said as he seated himself on his two walking sticks.

"Yes," I said. "I suppose Mrs Pressley is about your age?"

"Well no, as a matter of fact Ada is not my wife, she's my housekeeper and she's fifteen years younger than me, but you know, these days her gets that awkward and cantankerous there's no living with her. Only this morning I said to her, 'Ada, you'm getting most difficult, you'm on the grumble all day.' Of course, her goes out to work for a farmer or two, you know. Does a bit of singling, or helps at hay-making time, hop-picking and so on, but at the moment her's doing nothing at all."

He put his hand in his pocket and pulled out his pipe and proceeded to fill it out of an outsize tobacco pouch.

"Of course, her trouble is, there's not much money — no work, no money, that's what I said to her. 'You can't expect the best of everything when you'm not working, Ada,' I said."

I watched him as he placidly pulled at his pipe.

48

"Well, you both get a pension, don't you, Mr Pressley? It's not much I know, but with that and a good garden and you have got a well-planted garden, your rent is only five pounds a year, well at least you should not go hungry, even if Ada doesn't work, should you?"

He looked at me sharply. "I draws the pension, always does, can't trust Ada with the money. My word, if I didn't draw it on a Friday, her'd come home with about half on it and her wouldn't know where the other half was gone, if her went for it."

I took a dislike there and then to Mr Pressley.

"Hm, well, it seems to me Ada don't get much out of life, but by the look of your fat tobacco pouch you get your little comforts." With that I turned away and I know as I walked off he sat on those two sticks and glared at me. After he had gone I felt sorry I had been so outspoken. It was no business of mine how they lived, I told myself, and they had probably lived in a state of tightness for years off and on, and most likely anything I would say would not help Ada. I decided not to express my views to Mr Pressley again.

The days passed, and after the house had been arranged to my liking I gave up my time to help Father outside. My father talked of hay-making soon, and apple-picking time. He intended to sell some of the better quality apples, but there would still be plenty for me to use and store. Each morning I would have to go into the orchard and pick up what apples had dropped overnight to be put into a heap for cider-making later on. The eggs Aunt Lizzie had given me for the broody hens hatched out: seventeen chicks — some Leghorns, Wyandottes, Rhode Island Reds and a few cockerels. Father had now arranged to work for a gentleman farmer Uncle knew called Mr Dent for four days a week. While he was away he put me to digging up the grass in the patch of ground opposite the house. There were no idle moments and I was glad when a wet day came and I could stay indoors and do some cleaning. On the two other days, Father worked at home. But he never worked on a Sunday except to see to the feeding of the stock.

8

As we sat at dinner Father said, "If it's a good day tomorrow I'll be putting in a day for Mr Dent."

"I shall find plenty to do," I said. I thought of cleaning that had been neglected in order to get the gardens done.

Next morning the sun shone gloriously and Father left the house early. I piled the dishes into the scullery and started to clean upstairs. The calves had been put into the orchard before Father left, the pigs had been seen to and I had fed the old hens with their chicks. They were all alive, except one, which had fallen into a pan of water near the spout and had drowned.

The upstairs finished, I concentrated on the downstairs work and rolled the matting up off the living room floor and threw it out on to the yard ready for a good brushing. I looked at the clock. It was about ten o'clock and I felt a cup of tea would not come amiss. It was a matter of minutes before I was settled in the chair with a steaming hot cup of cheer.

The house seemed suddenly quiet. The birds usually singing outside in the trees seemed to have gone away. The sun shone strongly through the small living room window. Suddenly as I sat in the chair I heard heavy footsteps upstairs in the bedroom that was immediately over the living room, and which was my bedroom. The footsteps were like those of a man, walking in heavy nailed boots, the kind father wore.

I sat and listened, really too frightened to move. The footfalls sounded as coming through into father's room and to the top step of the stairs. The footsteps stopped. I had not long finished cleaning upstairs and to think anyone could have walked upstairs was ridiculous, yet, those footsteps upstairs were definitely those of a man.

I wanted to get up off the chair and walk to the door at the bottom of the stairs and look up, but I did not have the nerve to do so. I sat still and listened for the steps to either go back to the room from whence they had come or to walk down the stairs. There was no further sound. After a few minutes of silence, except for the ticking of the small clock on the mantelpiece, I went to the door at the bottom of the stairs and looked up, and then, slowly walked up the stairs to the top. I remembered then that I had fastened the door between the two rooms as sometimes it banged when the window was open. The door was still shut. I looked into the cupboard where I hung my clothes and under the bed, but saw nothing unusual. I returned to the living room and continued with my work, but my mind dwelt on what had happened. I thought too, of that night when we had had to sit on the stone wheel outside for hours until the dawn, because the key would not turn in the lock yet, since then, the door had opened and locked with no trouble, and had not required any attention.

That evening I told Father about the footsteps, and he was very annoyed. "You imagined it. How could there be footsteps?" he said. The matter was dropped but a month later I heard the footsteps again under much the same circumstances.

I needed company. I needed another woman to talk to, so when my father was away I would go over to the Jones's cottage and have half an hour's chat with Mrs Jones. I liked her, she was a clean, hard-working woman and a good mother. Sometimes she would make a quick cup of tea and sometimes I was offered a bit of cake. But if my father was around when I went to the village, I had to cut her dead, as I knew my father would disapprove.

I continued to go to Lil's to help make the butter. Every Thursday followed the same routine. I would lock the house and reach the farm at about ten. Lil would have got the wooden churn out; it was barrel-shaped on a strong stand and it had a six-inch hole cut out of the side through which the cream was poured in. The cut-out piece, wrapped in a piece of clean linen, served as a bung, to stop the cream oozing out. When the cream was in the churn Lil would leave me to turn the handle round and round while she went about her other jobs. But she would come back now and then and she could tell by listening to the swish of the cream how it was doing. After about an hour, the swishing would stop and I could hear thud, thud, as the butter was getting solid. "I should think it's about ready," Lil would say and she would pour off the buttermilk and add a few pints of fresh water, give the churn a few more turns, and the butter would be taken out and put on the clean damp surface of the table. After she had salted it, Lil would knead it, then pat it into half-pound oblongs, each with three marks along the top. "Everybody has their own way of marking their butter," she would say. It looked good and yellow. Then I would scald the churn out with boiling water from the large kettle over the fire, swishing the water round in it, while Lil continued to pat her butter. I always bought our butter from Lil. Never once did she give me half a pound, or make a pot of tea, or offer even a glass of cider. There was almost no conversation and I would leave when the job was done. Sometimes she would say: "How is things down your place?" and I would say, "Not too bad". But I got used to Lil's ways and expected nothing.

Once I caught sight of Mr Pressley's Ada. She was at the front of their cottage. She looked old, although she couldn't have been more than sixty-two or three, but I only glimpsed her through the hedge by the water spout.

It grew hot and the days passed without event. I would feed the chicks and collect the few eggs from the old hens and feed the five piglets. I was finding them tricky. As soon as I opened their pen door and before I could tip their feed into the trough they would come rushing out of their sleeping quarters to greet me, and with a pail in each hand it was difficult to stop them going into the yard. They were getting bigger and rougher every day.

I was tending my chicks when Mr Pressley called to me from the gate.

"They be a nice lot, Elizabeth, and no mistake," he said as he put his sticks firmly into the ground. I thought, any minute now he's going to plant his seat on those two handles.

"Yes, they're doing fine," I said.

"How old be they now?" said Mr Pressley, settling himself, as I thought, on the sticks.

"Oh, seven weeks old, I think, and the one old hen is back in lay already, I expect she will leave her chicks now — but they are big enough to look after themselves. I want Father to get me some more broody hens. I would like to hatch out some ducks, but he said ducks dibble the ground so, and are messy, I can have more chicks if I like — ducks he won't have."

"And how are the pigs?"

"Oh, fine," I said. "Father let them loose upon the orchard last night, but he won't do so again until they have rings through their noses, they dug up the ground a bit, so I can see me having the job of holding the little devils while the rings are put in. I'm not looking forward to that."

"That's nothing to worry about," said Mr Pressley.

"Mr Pressley, there's something I want to ask you," I said as I walked down the yard to the gate. "Did you know the people who lived in this house very well?"

"Well, yes, of course I did. He married and came straight into this house. We were neighbours for a good many years, but he lived here must be fifty years and was in this house long afore I came to live in my house. Then, of course he had children — let me see, yes, there was two boys, and hm, yes, three gells . . . "

"Yes, but did he die, not long before my father bought this place?"

"Well, you see, my dear, the old fellow worked here all his life. His wife worked too, the kids grew up, left home, married and it was generally supposed the old boy had money, but about two years afore he died, he went queer in the head and got on times a bit dangerous, sort of, and they talked of getting him put away in the asylum. Well, sometimes, he was all right, sometimes real bad in the head. Then one day he told the old gell, he said, 'You think I be mad, don't you? Well, I'll tell you summat, you're going to put me away, you thinks you're going to get my money, but you will never get my money — never.' It seems he had drawn all of his money out of the bank some good time before, without his wife knowing.

What he had done with it, they never knowed, but none of 'um had a penny piece, and the old lady lived on in the house about eighteen months after the old chap died."

"What happened after that, as regards the house?"

"Well, you know it was idle for six months, then Old Prosser, he was the landlord of these two properties, had them advertised, and nobody bought, then it was sold by auction and your Dad bought, as you know."

As I went on with my various jobs I thought a lot about what Mr Pressley had said. Could it be that somewhere in the house the old man had buried the money? Could it be that, if there are ghosts, the old man was coming back to look for it?

9

"The pigs need ringing," my father said. "I think I'll stay at home today, and we'll get those pigs done, first thing."

My father had got into the habit of letting out the two older pigs for half an hour in the evenings, and sometimes, he would sit out on the old stone wheel and when they came down from the orchard he would offer each pig a handful of corn. The pigs got used to this and they would take the corn gently out of his hand. But Father discovered they had been rooting up the grass in the orchard, so they had to be ringed.

My father straddled the pig, pulling his head back by its ears. When he shouted, "Now!" I was supposed to place the nail in the pliers and squeeze it into the struggling pig's nostril to form the ring. However, when my father was standing over the pig, he fell flat on his back and the pig scuttled out squealing for dear life. After a big tussle she was got back and rung, and also the second one, and a fortnight later, it was the turn of the piglets and my turn to hold them while Father ringed them. Only two were going to be done as the other three were going to be sold shortly in the market. They were now half-grown. I held on to the pig's ears while it made a terrible noise and the second pig squealed in sympathy, and just as my father raised the pliers I said I couldn't hold on any longer.

"Yes, you can," Father bellowed. With that the pig jumped ·forward, forcing me to let go of his ears, and I fell on my seat into the manure. I was up again in a second. It was no use brushing myself down, I was wet and sticky and shaken.

"Come on, you're not hurt. Try again. We have to get this job done." The second try was more successful and after some more gymnastics the task was done.

That afternoon I had to go down to the village for tobacco. My father was always running short of it. When he worked in the fields he chewed it, and in the house he smoked a pipe. One of my vivid memories of childhood is of when I was about eight years old and it was my father's birthday. He was sitting in his rocking chair smoking a clay pipe. I had a silver threepenny piece and I decided I was going to buy my father a 'churchwarden' pipe which was of clay and had a stem about ten inches long. I went out to the shop where I had seen them and bought one with my threepence and took it home to him. I badly wanted to see him smoke it and hung around for ages pleading with him to fill it and light it, but all he would say was, 'Yes, I will smoke it by and by.' Eventually I gave up and went out to play in the street. When I came back sometime later, the pipe lay broken. I never knew why, and it was never smoked.

On my way back from the village I met Mrs Jones, and I apologised for not having been over to see her.

"I shouldn't worry, dear," she said. "I have an idea your dad won't want you to mix up with us, the looks he gives my kids when he sees them. Hm, and the unfriendly glances he has cast my way when he has seen me doesn't make me feel we are very popular."

My face reddened. "Well, I'm afraid Father is a man who does not care for mixing with any people so it's not particularly you, Mrs Jones, and that is principally why Mother refused to come to live down here. She felt she would be lonely."

Mrs Jones nodded her head and the flowers in her hat wobbled. "It's all right with me, and I'm not one for gossiping," she said. "But your life is going to be lonely isn't it, I mean with just your father, there's no young girls round here for you to get friendly with. Let's see, the nearest is Old Maudie Lee's girl, hm, but they're a rum lot, I don't think you'll care for them."

"I don't think Father would approve of any girl's company for me, like he's always said — 'I haven't any friends, and I can't see why you want any.'"

"Perhaps one afternoon you will come over for a short while, to have a cup of tea?" Mrs Jones asked. I said I would.

Very soon we came to the bend of the road. I hoped very much that Father would not see me walking down the road with Mrs Jones. I knew that I could see our cottage clearly after rounding the bend and then I could see him quite plainly working in the garden. Any hope I had of him not seeing me was completely shattered for as we neared the lane that turned down to Mrs Jones's house he heard our voices and looked up. As he saw us saying 'goodbye' he stood up and rested his two hands on the handle of his fork, watching me as I walked down the road to the cottage. I opened the little gate and walked up the cobbled path to the porch. I placed my shopping bag on the porch seat and walked down the garden path. Any argument that was to be might just as well be got over with at once.

"I thought I told you not to mix up with the Joneses," said Father, glaring at me.

"Mrs Jones was coming home from shopping the same time as me, and I could not very well walk one side of the road and she the other side, so we walked down together seeing we are neighbours," I said quietly.

"I tell you I won't have it, when I say that I mean you to understand that. Now get in that house, an' don't let me see you in her company again," Father yelled the words at me. I decided there was no use in continuing any explanations. I still meant to see Mrs Jones and her family occasionally as I was very lonely. To me the country was beautiful, I loved the clean smell, the flowers, the lovely green leaves on the trees and everything that went with the country, but I lived a lonely life — Father away or home, to me it was lonely. It seemed it was wrong to talk to anyone. Aunt Lizzie had given me an open invitation to go to see her when I liked, but there had been too much to do and the four-mile walk of the return journey would have meant being away from the house too long. I had seen her only the once.

I went regularly to Lil every Thursday morning to help her make the butter and to help wash the dairy utensils but she seldom had much to say. I always felt there was some sort of barrier between us and I felt it difficult to make conversation. I found it always a relief when at last I could go. I felt she did not approve of me.

One Thursday when I arrived home after helping Lil, I thought I would walk up the road to the meadow to see if the cattle were all right. I then decided a cup of tea while I warmed up some lunch, would be very pleasing. When I got to the meadow I found the gate wide open and the cattle missing. I stood for a moment too frightened to move. I wondered how long they had been out, probably only a short time, perhaps over two hours. I had been away longer than that. I felt sick with fright. I decided that there was no point in going back along the road I had just walked but that it would be best to walk along the road to the village and go down the two side turnings hoping they might be there. The road was narrow, I had no hope of getting ahead of them if they had proceeded towards the village and could only hope that someone would be walking along the road wherever they were and be able to turn them back for me.

I got right into the village and asked several people I met at various times if they had seen two stray cattle, but no one had seen them. At last I turned back and on my way met the village policeman. I told him about the cattle straying off, gave him a description of them and he promised to let me know if he heard anything of them. I retraced my steps back home, hoping that somehow or other they had found their way back to the meadow. The gate was still wide open but the cattle had not got home. I decided to leave the gate of the yard wide open to give them the choice of either the yard or the meadow, should they get back with or without me.

I went to the end of the road where the lane to Lil's place led from, but instead of going up the lane I went straight along the road, past the thatched roof cottage on the corner, past two more on the right-hand side that were brick-built, with untidy-looking gardens and on till I came to a bridge where a fast flowing stream ran under it. At any other time I would have stopped to admire the bridge and the stream with a windmill in the meadow some two hundred yards away but I plodded on fervently hoping to see the cattle soon. Soon I was at a crossroad and wondered which road to take. I stood a few minutes and presently I saw a lad. I decided to stop him. I asked if he had come along the road for any distance and he replied, 'About two miles.' I explained I had lost two young cattle and wondered if he might have seen them. His reply was 'No,' so I decided to take another road. I walked a quarter of an hour before I met two little boys. I enquired if they had seen two stray cattle and they replied they had not.

I turned back along the road and decided I would make for home. I was about half a mile from home when I saw them, grazing quite peacefully on the side of the road. It was obvious they had taken a different road from me. I spoke to them as I went towards them and I slowly got behind them. Soon we came to the forked road. I watched them with bated breath hoping they would take the road to the right, which they did. I felt they would be no trouble now. The yard gate is open, they'll go in there, I told myself. I drove them very slowly when we neared the gate and stopped as they reached the open gate. The devil himself must have been in those cattle, they gave one look, then one of them decided to pass it, and the other followed. I now had no hope of getting ahead of them and prayed they would go through the open meadow gate but they passed that one too. Now my only hope was to see someone whom I could shout to stop the cattle going on. I was halfway to the village again before I met a lady and a little girl who had obviously been shopping. I called to her and between them they made the cattle stand. The two heifers turned towards home.

"I know where you live. You keep ahead and I'll come behind them," she called. "Is your gate open?"

"Yes," I shouted back. "I want them to go into the cowshed."

When we got to the yard gate they turned through it quite easily. I thanked the woman and told her what a relief it was to get them home. I told her of the miles it seemed to me I had travelled to find them. She said her name was Mrs Roberts and that she lived in the first cottage of the two I had seen as I went along the unfamiliar turning past the thatched cottage on the corner.

I left her and soon had the cattle fastened in the cowshed. I gave them water and decided they would stay there at least until I had had some food. The fire was soon lit and the kettle boiling. I was too hungry to cook anything and got the easiest thing to hand — some cold meat and bread. I glanced at the clock and found it was three o'clock. I had been nearly three hours looking for those cattle, I reflected.

Father's only comment when I told him what had happened was that I should not have been away from the house so long. I could only reply by saying it was necessary if I were to help Lil with her butter-making for me to be away two hours. I had been going to help with this job for three months and I felt the job would be mine for as long as I lived with my father. I could not imagine Lil telling me she could manage without me and I blamed Father in my secret mind for having promised my help in place of payment for my sleeping in Lil's house, for those two weeks. I disliked the obligation.

I had been with my father for about three months now and I didn't have a penny of my own. He gave me money for the groceries and the butcher, for paraffin and the occasional bag of coal, but that was it. My father was not generous and it was a worry to make ends meet. My mother wrote from Coventry where she was working but she never divulged her address. Her job was obviously going to continue until the war ended, so I decided that I had to make the best of it. I found the loneliness sometimes intolerable. My father and I had nothing in common and I had no-one to talk to but Mrs Jones. People in Dilwyn seemed cagy. If you met anyone on the road the most you would get would be a 'Good morning'. "Yes," said Mrs Jones, "until you've lived in this village a few years you're regarded as a 'foreigner'."

I still had visits from Mr Pressley who would stand out on the road by our big gate.

"Ada's not well. Got a pain in her stomach."

"Well, perhaps you ought to get the doctor."

"Oh no, can't do that, he charges five shillings if he has to pay a visit."

"Is there anything I can do?" I had to offer, even though I had only ever seen her at a distance.

"I ought to look for a nice young woman and get rid of Ada — she's only my housekeeper. I could do with a nice young woman — like yourself."

I left him standing in the road and went indoors shutting the door loudly. He was a filthy old man and he never washed himself.

I knew I would not be happy in Dilwyn. I could only hope that sometime, my mother would change her mind and come back to my father, and I would be released.

My father mentioned to Uncle Ted that we had a couple of perry pear trees and it was agreed that when they were ready we should pick them and Uncle would fetch the pears to make the perry in his cider mill. In return my father would give him two or three day's hay-making. I went too, while the men cut the grass with a scythe each (ordinary small farmers like my uncle could not afford machines), I was given a hayfork and it was my job to shake the grass out loosely so that it would dry. For two days and a half I walked the two miles up to Headland Farm to help with the hay and then, still in the heat of the day, walked the two miles home again, before my father left, so that I could see the calves were all right, feed the chickens, take water to the pigs and then get on with all the household chores, preparing the dinner of ham and vegetables. (Father had bought a complete ham from my uncle.)

It was shortly after this that Father announced that we must start our own hay-making. There was the meadow and the orchard to be cut, and once the grass was dry we would have to get it all into the big barn — about five hundred yards away.

The pig and poultry meal used to come in hundredweight sacks. I myself had opened one of these sacks and after beating out the meal that clung to it had washed the hessian and made a 'coarse apron' from it. People used them for jobs like feeding the pigs and chickens, and it was very useful when scrubbing the stone floor and on washing day. We opened up two of these sacks and sewed them together and attached two long sticks to either side, and this is what we used to carry the hay all the way into the barn. Thankfully the weather remained good for four days and it can be imagined what work it was to load the 'skip' as my father called it and drag it down to the barn, and it can be imagined how many loads we dragged in this way before the whole of the hay was gathered. There was so much hay that it reached up to the beams long before we had got it all in. Father said if I climbed up on top and trampled on it, it would go down quite a bit and to my surprise it went down a good way. It took two days of very hard work to carry in the hay. We were both very pleased when it was finished.

Father was cleaning out the pigpen one Sunday morning. "I don't like working on Sunday," he said, "but with one thing or another I've had no chance to get them done this week and they are in such a pickle — dirty little varmints." He wheeled the barrow out to start on the job straight away. He was about half-done when there came two men whom Father knew. He explained afterwards that when he went to work for Mr Dent these men were also workmen of Mr Dent's and they all three sometimes worked together.

"Don't let us disturb you, Bob, we never mind watching someone else work. Matter of fact, we don't mind work at all, long as someone else is doing it, not us. What say you, Jim?" There was laughter in which Father joined.

"Well, wait a bit while I get this last barrow load out, an' let me give these little pests a bit of clean straw, then I shan't mind giving you a glass of cider apiece." The three men went into the barn whilst Father called over his shoulder, "Fetch some glasses, Elizabeth."

I took the glasses into the barn and with a smile and a nod I left them. When lunch was cooked about an hour and a half later the men were still drinking cider and swapping yarns. I went out to the barn to tell Father. "I'll be there in five minutes," he said. I proceeded to eat my own lunch some ten minutes later when I could see Father was not coming for his, and placed his dinner to keep warm. An hour later the men went and Father was far from sober when he came into the kitchen.

"Your dinner is most likely spoilt. A dinner needs to be eaten when it's cooked. I expect the Yorkshire pudding is quite spoilt," I said, as I lifted the plate that covered his dinner. "You would have thought they would have taken the hint to go when I came out to tell you your dinner was ready."

"Never mind, never mind. I don't want any dinner anyway," said Father as he slumped into the chair. I put away the spoilt dinner and went out into the orchard.

The same thing happened for several Sundays after that, and I got very annoyed. Then I mentioned it to Father and he said next time they came he would cut the men short. The following Sunday they came again and when lunch was ready I went out to the barn to tell Father. I turned to the men and said, "For the last six Sundays I have cooked a dinner and for six Sundays my father has had his dinner spoilt and it's been uneatable when he has at last come home for it. Haven't you got a home to go to, if you have for goodness' sake go home to it and get your own dinner — then perhaps my father will have his properly for once." The men were sitting on the hay that was scattered about the barrel. Father was sitting beside the barrel but the two men scrambled to their feet at once, they looked as uncomfortable as I felt. I walked out of the barn and into the house. Father came into the house. He was furious as I knew he would be.

"Don't you ever do that again. Come out and say, 'Dinner is ready' and leave me to please myself when I come. I won't have you make a fool of me," he shouted.

"Look, Father, if this kind of thing is going on every Sunday I will not bother to cook dinner, it's a waste of time and good food."

"While I have to keep you, you'll do as I say and don't forget it."

"When I was in my last job I was treated decently and I was paid for my work. I have been here for over three months now

63

and in that time you have never thought it necessary to give me a shilling for myself. The money I came with I had to spend to get new boots because my other boots were spoilt walking through the flood water. I don't even have the money to buy a stamp," I said quietly as I faced him across the table.

"Oh, so that's what's the matter. I've caught you looking sulky a few times lately," Father said as he put his two hands on the table. "I see, I see, well perhaps you will remember the years I kept you and never got any money for it. But you come down here for just three months and you start to whine for money and what would you spend it on? Trash. That's what you would spend it on. And you'll just be happy without it, so there. I have none to give you and just one thing more. You'll just be decent to people who come to see me in future, or I'll be having a lot more to say." With this he slumped into the chair and ate his dinner while I tried to swallow mine and after a few minutes I pushed the plate away.

Later I sat in my bedroom and thought over the argument that had arisen. My father had never tolerated being 'answered back' by any of us. If he or Mother ever said anything, none of us children dared to contradict and I knew Father would not forget what I had said in a hurry. I had no idea my pent-up temper would be loosened in such a way but I had been feeling very downhearted because I had no money and had been wondering how I could bring the matter up in conversation.

Teatime came, not a word was spoken by Father or myself. Nor for several teatimes to come. I felt very lonely and wished Mother would come to live with my Father so that I could go away. I knew Mother would not stand for any nonsense like meanness over money.

10

As I was busy sweeping the yard Mr Pressley was walking down his drive towards the road. He glanced my way through the bushes.

"Good morning, Elizabeth, isn't it lovely today?" he said. I agreed. Then, in a moment, he was outside the yard gate. I walked down to the gate to speak to Mr Pressley.

"Oh Mr Pressley, have you cut your nose?" I said. I could see he had a piece of adhesive plaster across the bridge of his nose.

"No, I didn't cut it. Ada did it," he said.

"Oh dear, how did it happen?"

"Well, I've told you how awkward she is and quarrelsome. Well, this morning it started at breakfast. She wanted to go to the village. It's pension day, and her knows I allus gets the pension, it saves her going up there. Her said her wanted to go and draw her own and do her own shopping — and, well, one thing led to another and her threw a cup at me — you see the result." With this he lit his pipe and pulled vigorously on it. I kept silent.

I decided I would go up to Ada. I had never spoken to her. Perhaps a few minutes' chat would cheer her up. Later when I saw Mr Pressley go slowly up the road I went out on to the road with the intention of going up through Mr Pressley's big gate but I found it was fastened by a chain and padlock. I stood and stared at the locked gate in surprise. I noticed too that barbed wire was fastened along the top. I went up into the orchard. The hedge parted our ground from the Pressleys' garden. I went up level with the house and stood still. The Pressleys' door was wide open and I could hear loud sobs coming from inside the house. I called and the sobbing

65

stopped. But no-one came out. I walked away. I decided to go to Mrs Jones and tell her about Mr Pressley's nose.

"She's not his wife, she's just living there," she said. "Ada," she said, "belonged to a very respectable family, her parents are dead, died years ago but she was unlucky and got herself into trouble. Oh, that's twenty years ago must be, but anyway when she found she was in trouble her people threw her out. It was round winter time and she had nowhere to go so she went into old Pressley's pigsty and there he found her, baby and all. His wife was dead so he took her into his house and he let her live there."

"And what happened after the baby was born and she lived in his house? I suppose she had to go to work to keep the little boy?"

"Oh yes, her couldn't go home of course, her people wouldn't have her," said Mrs Jones. She was leaning on the door post and I stood on the step just below the doorstep.

"She went out to work for various farmers like she does now, taking the baby then, of course with her, but old Pressley used to always expect her to give up every penny she earned, as he said he was letting them live there. No, she has never owned anything. Many rows and fights there has been in that house over the money she earned and she has always had to give up every penny. Many is the time she has carried bruises from one of his sticks — yes, and from his boot; you see him walking on those two sticks, watching him you'd think he could not walk an inch without them, that's all bunk. He can walk as good as you or me, that's only so he can get more help from his clubs. He's nothing but an old hypocrite. If you heard her crying — then I suppose he has been hitting her about again."

The piglets, now half-grown, went to market. I had hoped that, when my father had sold them, he would give me a pound or two, but when he returned with a few drinks inside him, he took the money out of his deep pocket and counted the gold sovereigns out on the table, picked them all up and carried them upstairs. They were put in his wooden trunk and any hopes I had were blighted. Sometimes at night I would dream about the two little boys at Dr Armstrong's and that I was back with them, and I would wake up feeling sad. But I had come to realise that I would never be going back.

One morning after my father had left for work for the day I was busy round the house. It was hot, the sun was shining relentlessly on my back as I was weeding the little side garden of flowers. Suddenly the two calves in the orchard began to gallop, their tails straight in the air, and plunged straight through the hedge into the garden. In no time, the runner beans now six feet high and laden with beans were entangled in their horns; the potatoes in full flower were trampled into the ground, the peas were all broken down. Frantically, I opened the side gate then dashed through the house to run to the cowshed and open that door, in the hopes that the calves would go in. I turned round to see that the calves had come into the house. In the living room they knocked the chairs over and one of them had the tablecloth draped over its head and was mad with fright. But by leaving both doors open, I eventually got them out into the yard and into the shed.

As I surveyed the mess in the house, with the broken crockery on the floor I was shocked to see the old sow come trundling in through the back door from the orchard — in no time she was in the sitting room, where she tried to pass under the table, but the legs of the table were not high enough for her back to pass underneath, and she carried the table about four feet before it toppled sideways and fell. The noise of the fall frightened her, and she dashed through both doors out on to the yard. She made straight for the sty, and within a minute she was safely inside.

I went in the garden and surveyed the devastation with dismay. What a shambles! What would my father say when he came back? The lovely garden — some three-quarters of an acre — that we had turned from what was almost a field was totally wrecked. There was nothing I could do there. I turned away to the house and started picking up the crockery. The teapot, mercifully, had survived, with only a dent in it.

All day the tension mounted: what would my father say when he came home? I sat and wondered what I could do. Had I owned any money, I would have packed up my things and gone away rather than face my father's wrath, when he saw the garden, but I owned not a cent. I looked at the clock frequently, and wished time would not pass so quickly.

However, the day passed, and it was time for me to prepare dinner. I had not eaten since breakfast — I had not felt I wanted a thing. When Father was due home, I glanced through the window often, to see if he was coming. Presently I saw him walking down the straight road towards home. Usually he glanced over the hedge on to the garden as he walked. He did so this time, and stood still, staring at it. When at last he came to the house he pushed open the scullery door and shouted at me: "What in God's name has happened to that garden?" I told him.

"I don't believe you were in the house when it happened, you were off galavanting somewhere, and not here to see to things," he said as he walked forward and grasped my wrist. "That's right, isn't it?"

"I was in the garden doing the weeding, it was no fault of mine," as I tried to free my wrist I shouted back at him.

He loosed my wrist. "To think of all the work I have done in that garden. Now look at it." He sat in the chair and buried his face in his hands.

I knew how he felt but I could offer no sympathy. I had suffered enough all day.

The meal was put on the table and was eaten in silence, indeed not one word did my father speak to me that evening, or the next morning before he left for work. But when he came home from work that evening, he raved and stormed over the garden and vowed I was not at home when the cattle broke in. I listened in silence, that evening and many other times after that, until one evening he said: "It was the 'bree' got after them. The 'bree' frightened them." He explained that the 'bree' was an insect bigger than a bumblebee and it had a trunk about three inches long — it made a humming noise and went after cattle. Some people call it a 'hornet' and if it manages to get on a cow's back it sticks its trunk straight through the hide and sucks blood out and it leaves quite a lump. That was what caused the panic. "Good job you were here," he said. I was thankful at last I was no longer given the blame.

Father brought a pretty little white and brown puppy home. He said he had just left his mother. As I hugged him to me I felt he would be great company for me.

"You will have to take him out and show him the chickens, he must learn to live with them, and don't spoil him by hugging him. I've brought him home to be a house dog not a lap dog, put him down. Anyway, if he grows as big as his mother you won't be able to nurse him. He'll be too big."

"What breed would you call him?"

"I wouldn't know that but Mr Dent keeps foxhounds. This is one of a litter from one of the bitches but they are mismarked and he is getting rid of all the puppies. He offered me one so I thought you would like it. It will make a good house dog if you won't spoil him."

The days passed, the puppy grew. He did not take kindly to being fussed over and if I attempted to cuddle him he took it upon himself to be rough, biting and pulling at my clothes, and in the end I contented myself with talking to him, teaching him not to touch the chickens. He found that each time he went near them he was sharply smacked and scolded and he very soon learnt to let them alone, especially when one of the old hens went for him one day with neck feathers up and her two feet forward. My father said we must give him a name and after much thought we decided to call him Bruce. I found him a hard bone to exercise his teeth on but he much preferred shoes, boots, cushions and even the towels that hung on the rail in the scullery. Anything he could get at he did, until he became quite a problem, nor did he improve as regards scratching the small plants in the garden, much to Father's annoyance. Soon he was chained up outside all the time. He was a good watchdog. He seemed to hear footsteps before anyone was in sight and barked loudly.

"My dear, could you help me?" I was washing up the dishes in the scullery one morning and the voice came from the open door. It was an old lady.

"I live in the little cottage next to Mrs Jones, my sister lives with me but she's very ill, I'm sure, she does not answer me when I speak to her. Could you go for the doctor? I wouldn't worry you but I walk so slow and I feel he should come at once." I wiped my hands on the towel.

"Yes, of course I'll go, but who is your doctor? Where do I find him?" She told me and very soon I was away. When I found the doctor's house I was told he would not return until lunchtime. I explained what was required of him and I returned to the little old lady, Miss Tomkins, to say the doctor would be given the message when he returned home. She was looking out for me through the dirty lace curtains but left the window and had the door open when I reached it.

"Oh dear, I'm afraid he won't be in time," she wailed.

"Can I come and make you a cup of tea?" I said. "I don't suppose you have had one yet, perhaps I could help you tidy up before the doctor comes?" She invited me into the house.

"The house is very dirty, my dear. My sister has not been well for several weeks now and I've had it all to do myself and it has really been too much for me. You see, I'm eighty-five and my sister is eighty-one, we're too old to do much."

I suggested we went upstairs to make the bedroom ready for the doctor's visit; she agreed to this and very soon we were in the bedroom on top of the stairs where the sister lay. I walked up to the bed with the old lady but there was no movement from her. The sister was either asleep or unconscious.

"Alice, Alice dear, how do you feel? Could you drink a cup of tea?" said old Miss Tomkins. There was still no movement from Alice and only the deep breathing proclaimed that she was alive. I suggested to the old lady that we leave the sister rest, and I began to take rugs up off the floor to take downstairs to be shaken and brushed. Presently the room was passable, then I went down with the old lady and while she drank a cup of tea as she sat in the corner I cleaned the other two rooms. Before I went, she said she would go back upstairs to sit with her sister and I watched her slow walk up the stairs.

The dog was chained by the back door wagging his tail fit to drop off. I was so pleased with his welcome that I picked him up to cuddle and I was surprised that for once he seemed to like to be fussed over. Later in the morning I paid a visit to the Tomkins's household and found the doctor had been. I had hoped to have been there as old Miss Tomkins seemed very vague as to what he had said, but it seemed she was to leave her sister rest and when she woke up to give her anything in the way of food or drink she required.

Before returning to my own house I called on Mrs Jones to tell her about the happenings with the old ladies. At first she seemed annoyed that she had not been called in before me, but I explained it was very possible she had been visited by Miss Tomkins before me. She cooled down a little and said she had been down the garden putting clothes on the line so it was possible the old lady had called at that time.

Mrs Jones thereupon decided to pay a visit next door and between us we kept a watch on them for two days. The third day the old lady went to Mrs Jones early in the morning to say her sister had died in the night. Mrs Jones was really splendid and took over the responsibility of all things attached to the funeral. Even to writing to the only relation the old lady had — a niece who sometimes visited her from Leominster. After the funeral Miss Tomkins went to live with her niece but about six weeks later the niece wrote to say the aunt had passed away in her sleep. The house was put up for sale and was subsequently bought by a retired draper and his wife by the name of Willis.

12

Very soon it was time to pick our fruit. The trees were loaded with apples of the best kind: Blenheims, Cox's Orange, russets, and cooking apples so large that some weighed about twelve ounces. Father decided we would spend a day picking the fruit then ready, so accordingly we started one morning as soon as the sun had dried off the dew.

"Where are we going to put it all?" I enquired. "You can't put it in the barn where the hay is."

"No, that's a problem," said Father.

We eventually decided that some of it should go on the floor of the sitting room and some on the floor in my bedroom. Then, when there was a lorry-load Father would hire a lorry to take it into town. Father had been told by Uncle Ted that he had seen apples priced at nine pence per pound in the shops and that he would be quite prepared to sell his direct to shops at fourpence.

"Hm, yes," said Father. "But I do not suppose you will manage to sell all direct to the shops, in that case you'll have to sell to the dealers, won't you?"

"Well, yes, I suppose so, and what price they'll pay as middle-men, I would not care to guess at, would you?" said Uncle Ted, "but I shall try to sell what I can first of all to the shops and the rest to the dealers — and what I don't sell, apart from what fruit Lizzie puts away for future use, I'll just put into cider. I have a lot of pears I shall use for perry."

Some days later Uncle saw Father again and told him he had taken a load of fruit into the dealers and he had not done too badly as regards price, so Father ordered a man with a lorry to take a load of fruit in next day. Accordingly next morning lorry-driver and Father plus half a ton of best fruit departed for

Leominster and to the same dealer that Uncle had been to. The dealer offered Father a penny farthing per pound for the fruit, nor could he be persuaded to go any higher. Indeed he was quite indifferent and said he was not particular about having it but as Father had taken it in six miles to him he would take it off him to oblige him at that price. Father refused to sell and went round the various fruit shops and sold the lot for three pence per pound but it grieved him to feel the shopkeeper would make sixpence per pound profit over and above what he bought it for. However, as he had a ton more of fruit to dispose of without whatever quantity he would need for cider, he felt any price was better than keeping the fruit to rot, so another day about a week later he hired Mr Williams and his lorry to take a further half ton of fruit into town. He told me what happened after he had been on this journey.

"When we got into town, I decided to try the shopkeepers and managed to sell six hundredweight for two pence per pound, tuppence mind you, it didn't cover much more than Williams' charge to hire the lorry and himself. Then I was left with four hundredweight so I tried the dealer! He refused the lot at any price. 'Take it where you sold the rest,' he said to me, so up the town I went. The kids were coming out of school, I was so mad I told Williams to stop and I tipped the four hundred-weight on to the road. 'Here you are, kids, help yourselves,' I said to them. There was such a scramble and they were making short work of them, but not fast enough, for a policeman who must have been standing on the corner came up and said, 'Hey, what's this?' and took my name and address. Said he'd have to make a charge. That I was obstructing on the highway or something, so I suppose I'll have to go to court. Don't suppose the charge will be much."

"No, I don't suppose it will," I said.

"Well, then Williams said he would like to have a look in at the market seeing it was market day and I did not mind, my time was my own, so we went into the market. Well, there were lots of pigs, sheep and chicken and I saw the old sow I've got in the lorry outside and she has nine young uns, you'll see her when we get her and her family down and into the sty. Her's all bones but a bit of good feeding and she'll soon look good. You get some grub ready, I expect Tom Williams is as hungry as me."

While they were unloading the sow and her family, I placed bread, cheese and a piece of boiled bacon on the table, together with a large jug of cider. Father got two glasses off the cupboard and soon the men were tucking into a good meal. I went outside to have a look at the sow with her nine babies. They were all around her as she fed from the trough.

"She's skinny all right," I said aloud. The old sow raised her head from the trough and looked at me. "You're a skinny old woman and you'll take a lot of feeding to get fat," I said to her as I put my hand over the fence that kept her in. She was quite willing to let me rub her head, and I liked her. Every evening Father let her out to have a run in the orchard and to get away from her babies for a while and sometimes I loosed her out, under Father's orders, for a run during the morning.

"It'll do her good to get out from those young varmints now and again. They seem to think she's just a dairy, able to have milk on tap all the time and they don't need it all the time," said Father.

Mr Pressley came up to the field gate. I had not seen him for quite a while but had heard him talking to Ada when they were in the garden together. The air was quiet and little traffic on the roads so that sounds could be heard for quite a distance.

"I haven't seen much of you just lately, Elizabeth," said Mr Pressley.

"No, I have been very busy."

I could see the old fellow was quite ready to stand and yarn so as I did not feel like bothering with him I told him I had to get on, I had a lot to do and that I had the cattle to put out in the meadow. He did not take the hint.

"I was looking at your pansies, they'm pretty, but mine are better than yours. You might like to come and see them and see Ada some time, you have not met her. Perhaps you will come up tomorrow, she will be home. I shall leave the gate unfastened but as I must go up to the village before dinner perhaps you would come up about ten, then I'll go off about eleven o'clock?"

Next morning at ten I presented myself at the Pressley front door. Mr Pressley opened the door when he saw me. He called up the stairs, "Ada, come down. Elizabeth has called to see you."

A tall, angular woman came down the stairs and through the kitchen to the front door. She was very dark, probably from working out in the fields. Her skin seemed sunburnt. Her hair, mostly grey, was pulled into a tight bun at the back of the head, her skirt and blouse were black but so old that they seemed green in places. Her sleeves were rolled up to the elbows and her arms seemed browner than her face.

"Hallo, Ada, I'm pleased to see you," I said.

"I am pleased to see you," she said. "This is the first time I've seen you. Well, how do you like it down here? Would you rather be living in the town?"

"Oh yes, I would rather live in the town and I shall go back again if the chance ever comes. I mean, when my mother decides to come to be with my father again."

I looked up at the house. "Your house is the same as ours, I suppose. Two rooms up, two down?"

"Yes, that's right," said Mr Pressley, "but I sleeps down in the kitchen now, it's warmer for me and it saves me climbing the stairs."

The house looked dark inside, then I could see a heavy, dark brown blanket hanging from the ceiling to the floor; to keep out draughts, I thought.

"You have a nice shed there, haven't you?" I said as I gazed at a big shed attached to the side of the house.

"Yes, that's where I keep the wood and coal and old things I don't use now," said Mr Pressley, as he opened the door. I saw that the ground was hard and black. He had

76

spent a lot of time walking round in there over the years, the ground was as hard as the road. Then, I was shown the garden, the apple trees and the long pansy bed that stretched the full length of the top of the garden, nearest the house. There were pansies of every colour that pansies could be — large-headed navy ones that looked and felt like velvet, yellow and navy, various blues, some blue and yellow and some mauve.

"My, they are lovely, I don't think I have seen anything nicer in the way of pansies," I said.

Mr Pressley beamed. "I'm glad you like them." All the time Ada was there and smiling but saying practically nothing.

I turned to her. "Do you like flowers, Ada?"

"Oh yes, I do but they are not my job. I haven't time for gardening at home much, I have my work in the fields — I should have been at work this morning but I shall go after dinner as I have left it so late."

Very soon I left and I never saw Ada again. About three weeks later there was a terrible row up at the house. The door was open and the shouting came from inside. Then I heard the door bang. I saw Mrs Jones during the day and I mentioned that there was quarrelling going on in the Pressley household.

"Nothing can be done about it, they have quarrelled for years and she has still stayed there, even though the boy is now about twenty. Yes, must be all that. I expect it's over her earnings again, she's been working and he wants the money. He's an old devil, if ever there was one."

"I feel sorry for her, Mrs Jones," I said, as I turned to gaze up to the cottage.

"Well, so do I, but my dear, no one can do nothing about it, and anyway, he keeps that gate locked — you couldn't get up there, only through the door that leads out into the top fields and I'll bet that one is locked too."

I said I did not know there was any other entrance to the house until now and that is why I had never seen Ada about, I supposed. Mrs Jones agreed that Ada used that door quite a lot.

For weeks after everything was quiet at the Pressley household. I did not see Mr Pressley very often, sometimes I would perhaps see him twice in about three or four days, then perhaps as much as a fortnight or three weeks would pass before I saw him again.

13

Father announced that George Davies would be coming in two days' time to kill one of the pigs (not Sally who was in farrow). Uncle Ted would also be coming down to give us a hand. As the pig weighed near two hundred pounds, it would need me, Father and Uncle Ted to hold it while George stuck the knife into its throat. I had orders to go to the village shop and bring a bar of salt (which cost sixpence) and ask the shopkeeper how much saltpetre would be required to mix with the salt for curing.

Uncle arrived, then George Davies, a hefty man, walking with a staff. With Father they carried the big bench out of the scullery into the yard and I scrubbed it down. My father went into the sty and tied a rope round the poor pig's leg and fetched him out into the yard. The pig made such a noise squealing, and the other one squealed in sympathy. It seemed the pig to be killed knew that something dreadful was about to happen. You could hear both pigs squealing almost as far as the village. Eventually, after much struggling, the pig was hauled out into the yard, and George Davies stood with his knife gleaming.

"Get her up on her side on the bench, head this way towards me," he said.

It wasn't easy, but we managed it. I felt sick as I helped hold the squirming animal down. But Mr Davies was an expert pig-killer and he was quick, though the pig went on kicking for some time.

When it was quite dead it was laid on the straw that had been strewn thickly on the yard. The straw was set fire to, to burn the hair of the pig. As soon as the pig was burned to his satisfaction on one side, Mr Davies turned it over, with Father's help, on to its other side. More straw was heaped round it, then Mr Davies began scraping the skin clear of the hair until the old pig, though dirty, was hairless.

After this, we got it into the scullery and hung it by its legs from the beam, its head almost touching the floor, except for the pan under its snout to catch the blood. Mr Davies slit the pig from its throat to its tail. I put the pipes in a large bowl; the liver, heart and lard on a big meat dish.

"We'll leave her now," said George Davies. "I'll come down tomorrow and cut her up. And now, Mr Walker, we'll have a jug of your cider," and to me, "some bread and cheese."

Then we all four tucked into the bread and cheese and cider while the three men yarned about past deeds, especially pigs and pig-killing, and the probable weight of our pig.

After the others had gone, Father continued to be in a great frame of mind. He went out into the yard and gathered up the straw that had been laid out, and piled it upon the manure heap. Then he washed down the yard with a big bass broom and several pails of water, while I scrubbed the bench down.

When this was done I went indoors to prepare the evening meal.

"George says this pig is a good eleven score — that's two hundred and twenty pounds, she certainly looks good, but we've got to scrub her, you and me, after we've eaten. We must have her clean ready for George." So our work was not finished yet. Another two pails of spring water were used scrubbing the pig till she looked pure white, except for the black markings on her head. I did not say much. I was still shattered by the noise the pig had made, and the noise of the other one safe in her pen, and holding the pig to be killed. I hoped that I would never have to do that again.

Next day, George Davies came. And after a jug of cider, he sharpened his knives on Father's grindstone. I had got the big trestle table all scrubbed and cleaned in the dairy, well layered with salt and saltpetre.

"Right, I'll get started," said George Davies. As he cut the hams out, Father was ready to take each one off him and place them on the salt bed. I began to rub handfuls of salt into the hams and around the bone I rubbed in saltpetre as directed by Father. After the hams came the two front legs. These were put on the table awaiting my attention. Then the pig was lifted from the beams to which it was fastened and laid on clean sacks on the scullery floor. The floor was cemented. This pleased Mr Davies as he said, after cutting the pig's head off, he would require to use a chopper which he had brought with him. The pig was then cut down through the backbone.

"There," said Mr Davies, "is the best part of the pig, and the most expensive cut — nothing to beat a nice rasher of back bacon." He trimmed a few pieces of the fat meat off, to "leave it a nice shape," he said. The meat was carried into the dairy, ready for me to salt but first I placed bread, cheese and pickles on the table. Father said Mr Davies would expect it. Mr Davies picked up a piece of the fat meat trimmings that he had cut off, and took it into the kitchen.

"A nice culf of bread and this bit of fat meat and that will please me, with a glass of your very good cider, Robert," he said as he sat in the wooden armchair.

"But, Mr Davies, the meat's raw, would you like me to fry it for you?" I said, coming into the kitchen behind him.

"Lor' bless you, no thank you. I like it just as it is. That will go down as sweet as a nut," he said.

"My father says you are a bachelor? Is that so?" I said to Mr Davies.

"Yes," he said.

"Don't you find it lonely on your own? I mean, you have to cook, clean, wash, mend as well as being out tramping miles, don't you get fed up with it?" I said as I sat down to drink a glass of cider too, and was ready for a gossip.

"Well, no, I don't find it lonely. I have the old dog. I take her with me sometimes but her's getting old now and is not fond of walking too far, so her stays home quite happy till I get there. My washing and mending is done by old Mrs Prosser, the rest I manage quite well."

"Did you never want to marry, or didn't the right girl come along?"

He looked at me and grinned. "Well now, I'll give you

81

several reasons that might be the right one, and you can take your pick," said Mr Davies, as Father filled his glass.

"It could have bin that I never wanted to give a woman half a sausage, to cook the other half for me. It could have bin I courted several wenches and never found the right one, it could have bin the one I would ha' liked to wed, didna' want me, it could be that the kind of life I have lived, tramping miles like I do this forty year, would not be fair to a woman, 'cos I never knows when I'm going to get home, well, now, there's several reasons, take your pick and anyone on 'um could be right," said Mr Davies as he leaned back in his chair and laughed gently.

When Mr Davies had gone I went down into the dairy and rubbed handfuls of ground salt into the flesh and spread it out on to the table. This I did every day for the following few weeks, replacing the salt as it dissolved and ran on to the floor. At last the meat was considered cured. Meanwhile we had enjoyed the pig's liver for several days — it was good cooked with onions and herbs from the garden.

So, we were well off: we had our own pig meat, eggs and vegetables, Sally the pig was in farrow, Father was to take the calves to market and he talked of getting some more pigs about eight weeks old. Indeed at the next market day, Father sold the calves and bought ten young pigs, returning in high spirits and full of cider.

14

One morning, when I had been getting water from the spout to fill the copper, Mr Pressley walked down to the gate and, settling his bottom on his two sticks, proceeded to light his pipe.

"Elizabeth," he said, "I want to talk to you."

"I'm very busy this morning. I'm getting the copper on the boil for washing. Is it important?"

"Well, yes, it is. I wants you to ask your father if he will put a new fire grate and a new oven in ma kitchen, the one we has is very old, and the big shed needs retiling. Nothing has been done to that house for years, and I needs a new grate."

"How long have you lived in that house, Mr Pressley? As you know, my father has owned it for less than a year."

"I've lived in it for fifty year and more, and things don't last for ever. I pays my rent regular as you will find — when it is due in a month's time, it will be there on the day. Will you tell your father what I said?"

I got all my washing done and then decided to make some brawn out of the pig's head (Mr Davies had chopped it in half), but I didn't know how to do it, so I went down to the village shop where I had to buy some more meat-hooks anyway.

"Look, I'll give you a cookery book," the shopkeeper's wife said. "I've got two, so you shall have one to keep."

I was so pleased. "This will give me something to read. I get so fed up at night-time. I have nothing to read, and I miss the daily papers we used to have."

She said she had plenty of books, novels and whatever, and so saying she disappeared into the other room and reappeared with the cookery book and three or four others.

I was very happy to feel that I had something to look at in the evenings.

After supper I decided to tell my father about Mr Pressley.

"These two houses were built at the same time. I have it down in the deeds. There's nothing wrong with *this* grate, is there?" my father shouted.

I had to admit that was so. I had blackleaded it every Saturday — a fire grate that must have been well looked after by the previous tenant.

"He's a dirty old skunk, he is filthy, with that old army coat with the brass buttons cut off, that old cap with the piece of a blanket sewn into it, hanging down his shoulders like a curtain, and that blanket fastened over him with safety pins. I want him out. While he is there in that house I will do nothing. His rent is two pounds ten shillings for six months, do you realise? That is one shilling and tenpence a week, and he wants me to spend about fifty pounds on that house. If I hear any more of this I'll give him notice when he pays his rent."

"All right, Father. Don't go on at me. I'm just telling you what he said."

"Well, you tell him he can get out," Father said and banged his fist on the table. After which he puffed his pipe in silence, while I looked at my books.

The cookery book proved to be an extravagant one. 'Take two glasses of wine . . . ', but I found my recipe for brawn. I got half the pig's head and, because it had lain in salt for some time, I let it soak for a couple of days in a bowl of water. And when I had made the brawn, my father was pleased, but he never mentioned Mr Pressley, though I knew he hadn't forgotten.

Meanwhile I hatched a plan to go into Leominster one day when my father was at work. I had never been to Leominster since I had been with my father and I just wanted to see the shops — and people. I figured it out that I could walk the six miles in less than an hour and a quarter, spend perhaps one hour just looking at the shops — I had no money to spend anyway — and I could do it all in three and a half hours. It was risky, I felt, but my father would not be home until five and if I

84

went soon after he left for work I could be back in time to feed the pigs. I knew that one of these days I would do it.

Every Thursday I made my way to help Lil with the butter-making. I had been going wet or fine every week for eight months. Sometimes she gave me a bottle of milk to take home. The cream had already been taken off, even for their own use, only skimmed milk was used.

When visitors were expected, a jug of fresh milk was put away from the morning's milk on the cool larder stone shelf. I was not considered in the light of a visitor, so when I was sometimes given a cup of tea, we both had tea with milk that had been carefully skimmed. Lil made cheese too, for the house use, with skimmed milk; whether it was good or not I never knew, as I never tasted it. She always wore the same shabby black skirt and black blouse — I never recall seeing her in anything different. I could only think she was 'very careful'. The bright spot about this Thursday journey was that I nearly always saw old Mr Benson, who lived at the white cottage with the thatched roof, that was on the corner of the road where I turned left to go to Lil's.

I always left home at the same time each week, so I could be home by lunch-time. I believe old Mr Benson had timed me along the road, for he was always outside when I passed. When his wife heard our voices she used to come out as well for a chat. She was quite old, I felt. When you are nineteen anybody over fifty strikes one as being 'old'. I always thought her beautiful, her skin needed no complexion aids, but it was her eyes that to me were the most beautiful. They seemed the eyes of a saint, when she looked at me, but into a world far beyond me, where there were pastures of beauty far beyond the beauty of the earth. I have perhaps a description that may puzzle the reader, I can only hope that I can be understood, for Mrs Benson had the face and eyes (at least to me) of a saint. I always enjoyed a few minutes' chat with them both, and would have minded very much if I had not seen them.

This time when I got home I was surprised to see the village policeman standing at the gate.

"Miss Walker?" he queried.

"Yes, is there anything wrong?" I asked, feeling quite startled.

"Why no, I've come to deliver a summons for your father to appear at Court at Leominster in a fortnight's time."

"I will give it to my Father when he comes home, he's at work and won't be home until evening. Will this be serious?"

Police Constable Willis smiled. "No, it's for dumping his apples in the street and causing an obstruction. About five bob and costs, it won't be much more, nothing to worry about."

The pig we killed was now fit for use. Every morning for three weeks it had been my job to go into the dairy, and thoroughly rub salt into the bacon, especially round the bone. The salt that had been rubbed in the previous day would a good part turn to 'brine' as Father called it; this would run off the bacon on to the table, and from there into the cement floor where it was swept up and thrown away. The floor was permanently wet during the salting period. Father had fixed hooks into the oak beams in the dairy, and the bacon was hung up to dry. The window space had no glass in it, just iron bars, so that plenty of fresh air circulated through them.

Father said that Sally the sow would be having her litter of young pigs in about two or three days' time, and, as he was going out to work that day I was to loose her out to take a walk up the orchard, and clean her bedding out, lay in plenty of clean straw in her sleeping quarters, clean out all the other quarters in her yard and slosh two or three buckets of water over the pen, which was cobblestone laid. Sally was a really quiet creature and she loved you to talk to her, and rub her back. I got into the habit of singing a song round the place, 'Sally O'Malley', and the old thing knew that, and whenever I let her loose, I only had to sing 'Sally O'Malley from the evergreen valley' and she would come trundling down from the orchard and walk behind me into the pigsty, and I always had a bit of 'special' in the pail for her and she knew it. I really liked her.

So I cleaned out her pen. Afterwards I had to clean my boots off, with a small brush dipped in water, before I could go inside the house, after which I rubbed off some of the water with an old rag. I studied them. I had bought those boots for a pound from the village shop five months ago. They had needed mending at the cobbler's in the village but I had had no money to get them repaired and I had no other boots to wear while they were being repaired. Now, I considered them past repairing. The soles were very thin — I could feel every small stone I trod on and we lived on a rough unmade road and the yard was no better. Five months' wear, every day, had done them no good. I knew I would have to speak to my father. Of course, I had my best shoes but I would never wear them round the farm, or hardly ever to the village. Two days' trailing through the mud would have finished them off for good.

Father seemed highly pleased with himself. He had seen a farmer, a friend of Paul's who, he thought, might buy the two yearlings. I was very pleased also, they had given me much worry, and I would be glad to see them go.

"He'll be coming down on Sunday to see them, and if he likes them he'll collect them on Monday, but I shan't be able to help him get them home. We're pretty busy at work and I can't be spared to stay home for the day."

"But surely he'll bring someone to help him — perhaps he has a boy of his own, or perhaps he can get a neighbour's boy?" I said in surprise.

"Well, we'll see when he comes, I suppose if he did buy them and me being at work, you won't have the cattle to bother about here, so I don't see it will hurt you to help him take them home."

I got up from the table, I felt the colour come to my face. "Father, I'm sorry but I'm not going to go driving cattle along the road with a stranger."

"He's a nice fella, I was talking to him — arranging about his coming to see the cattle, it will be all right, and you'll be glad enough to see them go. It will give you more time to gossip with Mrs Jones and old Pressley, so you *could* help him take them home," said Father rising from the table and standing on the mat a foot or so from me.

"You make it plain to this man he'd better bring someone with him; I'm not going." I proceeded to carry the dishes from the table.

"Put those dishes down and listen to me," Father said. I put the plates back on the table. "You did not come down here willingly, and you have never tried to make yourself happy. Everything you do, you do grudgingly. I had hoped your mother would have been down by now, but until she does come you will stay here."

As my father had spoken so plainly, I felt I must brace myself and tell him my side of the story.

"I came down here feeling it was my job to come and look after you. I'll admit I did not like leaving a good job with good people, but I came down with every intention of doing the best I was able, and I have tried," I said quietly. "You pledged my help to Lil for her butter-making because I slept at her house for a fortnight, and now after all these months I'm still going there, and if I'm here ten years she'd still expect me to tramp up there, wet or fine. She doesn't feel she owes me anything, and she scarcely thanks me.

"Since I've been here, how much money have you given me — I mean for myself? None, and now look at my boots." I tore my boots off my feet. "Look at them; only this morning I put fresh cardboard inside to cover the hole in the sole. I spend a good part of the day when it's wet with wet feet, or running round the house barefoot, while I dry my boots. How can I be happy here, with no money to buy boots? Then I must be alone, I must not talk to a soul, only if it's to Lil, or Uncle Ted or Aunt Lizzie when I see them, which is not often. I'm alone except for when you are home, and often don't speak to a soul for days. But, let that pass; it doesn't matter. I am sure Mother would never come down here and lead my life." I picked up the plates and walked to the scullery. I put them down and returned to the kitchen. "I hope you will make it quite plain to the man who comes to see the cattle, that he must make his own arrangements to take them away."

Father sat down again on the chair, and held his head in his hands. "Never would I believe that one of my own children would talk like this to me," he groaned.

I walked quietly past him, picked up my boots, replaced the cardboard and put my boots back on.

"Haven't I always done everything for you all my life? Haven't I always kept you clothed and fed, haven't I always done my duty by you? And now look at you, standing there and defying me," Father shouted at me.

"I suppose you have done all you think you should have done. You brought me into the world, but you and Mother would rather you had not had me at all. I just happened along but by the time I arrived there were four before me. You did your duty and Mother too, according to your ideas. Tell me, do you ever remember our stockings filled at Christmastime? Do you, Father? We all hung our stockings up hoping something might be dropped inside, but every Christmas morning they were quite empty. The elder boys didn't mind much, they were working and could buy something for themselves." I paused for breath, and when I spoke again I lowered my voice. "There was just Walter and me; you were working every day, but there were no Christmas presents for us.

"Do you remember the time John put a lump of coal in Walter's stocking? We dashed downstairs, Walter and I, thinking perhaps this time we might be lucky. Walter saw the bulge in his stocking and he was so delighted, but when he put his hand down his stocking all he found was the lump of coal. He cried so much, he was sick. About the beginning of December, Mother used to say, 'If you don't be good you'll get nothing in your stocking for Christmas'. We would try to be very good, but it made no difference, good or bad we got nothing, not even an orange and a packet of sweets!

"I remember I used to go out into the street, all dressed up in my Sunday dress, only to see all the neighbours' kids dressed up, and playing with their toys. I could only look on, and hope

I might be allowed to play with their toys too. There were children poorer than we were, with fathers who could never pass the pub at the bottom of the street. Yes, and often stopped there so long that half their pay was gone before they went home. But somehow their kids had toys for Christmas; Walter and me — nothing. I was glad to leave school and go to work. Then the Pettigrews told me you had said I was not to be allowed out. I was happy at the Armstrongs, I loved them all, but I gave it up to come to keep house for you. I do not find it very nice to own no money. If you had only given me a few shillings a week, I could have saved it to buy the things I needed."

I looked at Father, then when I stopped speaking he raised his head from his hands, and sat up straight.

"Now that you have got that off your chest I'll tell you something," said Father quite calmly now. "You know your Uncle sent to tell me he had heard of a little place down here that might suit me. I got special leave from my work at the pit to come down and see it. I liked it, but I knew I had not enough money to buy it. Your Uncle offered to help me out, and with his help I was able to pay for it. I did not want old Pressley's cottage, but the two cottages were to be sold together, so I bought the two. Well, since then he has been pressing me for the money. Says he's short — maybe it's the boys are anxious to see him have the money in, I don't know, but I have been paying him when I can. When the cattle go, if this man don't buy them I shall sell them elsewhere, I shall give your uncle that cash, except that I shall buy two young calves out of it. The rest he shall have. I wish to get him paid off on my own account, and that is why I am short of money."

I had had no idea Father had borrowed money to buy the house, though I suppose I should have been surprised that he could have accumulated over the years (having brought up a family) enough money to buy the properties, but I had not given the matter any thought at all. As it was I felt sorry about my outburst, and although I made no apology I did all I could to be sweet, even making up my mind to help take the cattle if need be.

However, when the farmer came on the Sunday to see the cattle he brought a lad with him. He was pleased with them, the price was settled, and they were taken away. I breathed a sigh of relief at their departure.

15

Life was happier now, after the little row I had had with Father. I tried to be more settled and I think he was nicer and I had not had to go up to the Headlands Farm or to Paul and Lil's for some time. I was home, in our own place, and things were manageable. Sally had had nine piglets and all were doing well. The dog, however, never let off his chain which I knew was bad for him, was not safe to be let loose. He would snap at our hands when we put his food in front of him. My father could only clean out his kennel by giving him a bone while the job was being done. I longed for a dog that I could make a pal of, one I could talk to, and I so often wished my father would get rid of Bruce.

I had not seen Mr Pressley for about three weeks. He had his sticks with him as usual, I had believed he was never without them, and could not walk without them, seeing how he leaned on them so heavily, except that I had been told previously by the post-mistress that one day he had been in to draw Ada's and his pension. To sign his name, he had propped the two sticks up against the counter. He carefully put the money in his purse (Mr Pressley always used a purse, no loose cash in trouser pockets that might fall through an unsuspected hole for him). Then he turned and walked away from the counter of the village shop, out through the door and straight to the pub, which was right next door. The next customer saw the sticks and mentioned them to the post-mistress, who had said, 'Why, they're Mr Pressley's.' With a chuckle the man, who knew Mr Pressley well, put the sticks behind the door. Some two or three drinks later, Mr Pressley left the pub and walked off down the road still minus his walking sticks, and it is said he had gone a good distance towards home, before he had missed them.

This morning he was putting his weight on the sticks quite hard — but, even so, his progress was very slow indeed. However, it was the appearance of Mr Pressley that shook me. The curtain of felt fixed to the back of his cap was hanging down to his shoulders, to keep the wind away from his neck. Round his middle he had a dark brown blanket wrapped tightly, and fastened in place by a large safety pin. It reached down to the top of his boots. He looked as if soap and water had not touched him for days.

"Hallo, Mr Pressley, are you cold?"

"Hello, Elizabeth, yes, I'm cold. I havena' been to bed all night, I've sat by the fire; and I'm not well," he said.

I said I was sorry to hear he was not well, and added, "Why don't you go to bed, Ada will look after you, you know."

"Well, you see," Mr Pressley paused, "Ada's not here, she's gone."

"Gone? Where's she gone, when did she go?"

"Well, her went about three weeks ago." He fumbled in his pocket.

I said I should have thought he would have come down to see me to tell me before.

"Should I have come to tell you ma business?" said Mr Pressley. "Her and I had a row over money as usual, her had a week's pay, an' I said her should give it to me towards expenses. There was an awful row, the language her used to me my dear. The most filthy language you ever heard. 'Ada!' I said. 'Ada don't use such language to me. I be an old man soon to die, and I don't want such talk in front o' me.' I tell you Elizabeth, it grieves me to hear such talk."

For a moment there was silence, then I asked if he had any idea she was going to walk out. He said he did not know that she would leave. They had had their quarrels he said, like most people, and the quarrels had been mostly about money because she was selfish, and was never willing to help pay expenses.

"Does her son know she's missing, at least that she's no longer with you?" I asked.

"As far as I know he do not, leastways I havena' told him. Her's gone, crept out on the house like a thief in the night, an' I'm not caring, I tell you I don't care."

"Oh, she went in the night," I said.

"We'd had an argument, see, and later on I went to bed, her often stayed up after me, an' I thought nothing about it. I must ha' fallen off to sleep, and didn't wake till morning. Then when I woke in the morning I called out to her, but got no answer. I got up, and found her had gone."

I asked if she had taken clothes with her, to which he replied he did not know. After some talk, in which I pressed him to communicate with her son, he left.

When Father returned that evening, he said he had called in to Mr Williams to book the lorry for the Tuesday. He said as he had to go to court, and it being market day they would take some of the pigs, and as the lorry would be empty he might, if the prices were right, bring back a few more pigs with him.

"And," he added, leaning his elbows on the table, "we'll pick up those young cockerels that is out there and sell them. There's no point in keeping them, I reckon there's six out there. If they go you'll have eleven pullets. How about me buying some young ones, about eight to twelve weeks, say about twenty?"

I said if Mr Williams had crates, perhaps he could lend them to us to bring the chickens back home in, I thought it would be a good idea — and that it would be just as easy to feed twenty or thirty more, since I had to feed the others. The matter was settled, and Father was in no way worried about going to court. He said the case was only a trivial one, and he thought it would not come to more than ten bob. But somehow I could not stop worrying about old Ada. I knew that the Pressleys' quarrels were not always verbal ones, and that they had on more than one occasion resorted to blows, but there was nothing I could do. There was no reason why she should not go away, when she felt she could put up with no more, I kept telling myself.

Father's workmates from Mr Dent's still came on Sundays

to spend the mornings drinking cider in the barn. It was so regular that sometimes Father did not seem to want them so often, but did not care to say so.

About two Sundays after we had sold the cattle Father and his two friends were seated round the barrel, and Father mentioned he had sold his cattle and was on the lookout for a couple of weaned calves to take their place. They had not been long there — possibly an hour when a man called. He said he was Mr Holland, and lived in the farm where the windmill was, Windmill Farm, and asked did I know it. I said I did, as I had been down past there the day that the two cattle had strayed. I asked him to sit in the kitchen while I called my father, whom I found sitting near the barrel on the hay.

"There is a man called to see you, Father."

"What does he want, do you know?"

"No, I don't, you'd better come and see for yourself," I replied.

Father got up and said, "Well, come on lads, we'll call it a day."

"It's all right, Robert, you go and see your business through, we'll wait here for you, we wouldn't wish to interfere with your business, would we, George?" said one of the men. Father stood a moment. "No, come on, I've got work to do anyway, away you go now, the old barrel will be empty soon enough, without making a party every Sunday."

The men got up off the straw reluctantly, and left the barn with Father following. He said he would be seeing them on the morrow at work, and they left.

Mr Holland was sitting by the fire. "Mr Walker, I've been talking to your nephew Paul Walker, of Beacon Farm, and he said he understood you might be buying some young calves, and I have some for sale. Thought maybe you'd like to see some that I have. I know this is Sunday, so maybe you do not care to do business on a Sunday; in that case you might come to see them any time during the week, as long as I know, so's to be there."

Father decided to go that very afternoon, and offered Mr Holland some cider, which was accepted. And after dinner,

Father went to see Mr Holland's calves and came home very pleased with himself, and the Hollands. It seemed Mrs Holland was 'a very nice woman, and a good looker too.' Father said she had made a great fuss of him, and had invited him into her kitchen. He had arranged about price and collection, which was to be on Monday. Father gleefully said he would not have to bother now about calves when he went to court at Leominster on Tuesday; he would now go into the market to buy only some pigs if the prices were suitable, and more poultry maybe.

"Could you take me in with you?" I asked. "I have never seen Leominster since the day you met me at the station. Do you think I could come?"

My father looked at me, shocked.

"Of course you can't come. What on earth do you want in Leominster? It wouldn't be nice, you riding on the cart. Besides, someone has to be at home to look after the place. No, gell, you can't come in with us, not today."

16

My father was doing the hedging. I was busy in the house. I had put in quite a lot of time pickling our own onions and had made several pounds of jam. For that I used a cauldron. As it was mostly wood I put on the fire, a saucepan would have slipped down the grate and been dangerous, but the cauldron could hang safely over the grate on the stay. I was spending the morning writing out labels to stick on the pots when there was a knock at the door. It was George Davies standing, smiling, with his long pole in his hand and a bag slung over his shoulder. He said he had just come from Paul's place where he had been to kill a pig and he had a message from Paul to Father. "Paul says he is going to plough up his potatoes on Wednesday and he wondered if your father would spare you to come potato-picking and bagging for a couple of days. I was to mention it to your father."

I stood for a moment with my back turned to Mr Davies looking through the window, then I said: "Mr Davies, if you didn't see my father — or me — you could not give the message, could you?"

"Well, no."

"Well," I said. "Could you just think no-one was in when you called? The truth is, Mr Davies, I come down here, leaving a very good job, to look after my father, and look after him I do, but I do object to my father loaning me out to the family when they need help — I am not asked if I mind. I'm just told, your Uncle wants you for a couple of days. I have helped my uncle with hay-making and he expects me to go cider-making shortly, and I have helped my cousin for weeks on butter-making already." I burst into tears. "I'm not used to this kind of life and I'm wondering just how much more I can stand."

"I won't tell a soul I've been," George Davies said, and with that he left.

Ada Morgan's son came to see Mr Pressley, after the old fellow wrote to him to tell him that his mother had left the Pressley household. It seemed, so Mr Pressley told me, the young man had no idea where his mother could be, and he was obviously very worried by the letter from the old man.

When Mr Pressley first told me of Ada's disappearance, I told Father what he had said, but he considered the matter as trivial, saying it was possible she had got a job somewhere, and did not wish the old man to know where she was.

I told Mrs Jones about it a day or two after Mr Pressley had told me. She took a different view to Father. It seemed Mrs Jones, having known Ada for years, felt pretty sure that the first thing Ada would have done, if she intended going away, would have been to let her son know. I suggested Ada had not had time to write to him perhaps. Mrs Jones then remembered that Ada could neither read nor write, "but", she said, "I feel she would have found some way to let him know.

"Do you know, I have an uncomfortable feeling that things are not as they should be. Old Pressley is an old devil, even though he's smarmy and all smiles when he meets you, but I know her life has been anything but happy, since he gave her a roof over her head. She has paid, yes and paid, all the twenty years she has been there," said Mrs Jones.

We agreed there was nothing we could do; things could clear perhaps in a few days.

Father came home with the calves on the next day. Mr Holland helped him to bring them, and he called out to me to have a look. They were very pretty, with white heads and four white hocks, both heifers marked the same. Mr Holland remarked with a laugh that in next to no time I would be able to start milking. A great friendship developed between Father and Mr Holland, who would often spend an hour in the barn with Father.

Father had done better than he had hoped at court, and had been dismissed with a caution. When he came home, he came home with the lorry loaded with six young pigs, in place of the five he had just sold, and forty young pullets, about four months old. He and Mr Williams had, before coming home, visited the tavern in the town, and neither was very sober. All the same Father had found time amongst his other activities to visit several of the shops with a view to selling his remaining fruit which was now ready for picking. The shopkeepers were very independent, saying that they had had so many offers of fruit. The price they offered for such fruit as Blenheims, Cox's Orange Pippins and many other kinds would not be worthwhile to hire the lorry to take the fruit in, so it was decided to shake it down from the trees, except for the quantity I wished to keep for winter use, which would have to be hand-picked. The rest could go for cider-making. The cattle and pigs came in for a fair share of the apples. We settled into fruit-picking the following week. The weather was dry and warm, and by the weekend we had finished the job. I had no place to store the fruit except in the sitting room on the floor, so I placed newspapers and meal sacks on the floor, before putting down about five hundredweight. Father protested that that quantity was far too much to keep, but I knew what was not kept would go into cider, so I had no qualms about robbing Father of a few gallons. The rest of the apples, after being shaken down from the trees, were carried in buckets, and tipped out into a large heap not far from the orchard gate, ready to be hauled up to Headlands Farm, when Uncle was ready to make it up into cider.

We had, too, cider apples in abundance. Father had arranged with Uncle to make his cider for him and when the cider was made there were three 'ogsheads or three barrels each holding a hundred gallons and also a small eighteen-gallon barrel of the 'primest stuff', Father said. I was sent off to spend two days helping to make the cider with Uncle Ted. The apples had been taken up to Uncle's farm by lorry some days before and they had been tipped off the lorry into a heap on the ground.

The first day I went up on the cider-making session I started off before nine o'clock. I was pleased to see Aunt Lizzie again. I had only seen her about twice since the day Father had taken me up to see her the first time.

"Ah, there you are, gell, nice and early to make a start at helping me to make the cider. Go and take your coat off, I hope you have brought some sensible boots with you. You're going to do quite a lot of walking this morning."

I said I had. Aunt Lizzie turned to me. "By and by we'll have some bait. Bit too early yet." Uncle gave me two pails.

"Here you are. Take these buckets, here's a spade. Fill the buckets with apples and then you take them into the cider mill. Here's the cider mill." We walked into a big shed. "You puts the apples in this trough, I'll go an' get the old hoss."

When I went to the apple heap with the two buckets the apples were covered quite a bit with leaves from the overhanging branches of the trees and quite a few snails were crawling on the fruit too. I proceeded to pick up the apples by hand, I didn't seem to make them stay on the spade. To me it seemed as bad as trying to eat peas off a knife.

"Get that spade under them, gell, it's easier," said Uncle.

"Well, you don't want the leaves picked up with the apples, do you, Uncle? I thought it would be better to pick them up by hand so as not to pick up leaves and these horrible old snails," I said as I straightened.

"Aye, that's all right. Put 'um in leaves, snails and all, it won't matter. It will all work out when the cider is in the barrel, you'll find."

I was nevertheless careful and pushed the leaves off the apples with the spade as I filled the buckets. When the circular stone trough was filled to suit Uncle Ted he fixed the horse to an arm that came out from inside the circle. This contrivance was loose and made from wood and it worked with the stone wheel attached to it. The stone wheel crushed the apples as it was taken round and of course as the horse went round in a circle outside the stone trough so the wheel crushed the apples. To the apples Uncle Ted put two buckets of water from the pump.

"Now then, gell, this is what you do," and he had a plank about four foot long, and about half an inch thick by about five inches wide. "You follow behind the old horse and as the wheel goes round with her, keep a little distance behind her and you rake the apples loose with this plank. The idea is that the apples must be well pulped. Now on you go, let's see how you do it."

I did exactly as I saw him do and he said, "That's right".

Round and round I followed the old horse raking the apples loose, but every now and then I would say 'Whoa' to him and we'd both stop a minute or two for a rest, then on we'd go again. The stones underfoot were very uneven and what with walking round so much on them I was glad when Uncle came in about an hour later and said, "Let's have a look now, and see how we be doing." I stopped a moment while Uncle stopped the horse. "Hm, wants quite a bit more, but go in the house now, Lizzie's getting a bit of bread and cheese ready for bait," so saying he loosed the horse and took him to the stable.

"How are you going on out there?" said Aunt Lizzie as I entered the big low-ceilinged kitchen.

"The first lot is not pulped enough so Uncle said, so I'll continue after bait. He said I was to come in."

"Oh yes, well, sit yourself down. I'll go and draw off a jug of cider." So saying she left the room, returning with a quart jug, brimful. I thought of the apples I had shovelled up with snails on some of them and somehow I could not fancy the cider.

"I'll have some water, Aunt, if you don't mind," I said as I picked up my tumbler and made for the pump.

"Water! Water!" roared Uncle Ted. "Why water? I thought you liked cider?"

"Well, yes I do — but I think I'll have water now, you know they say it's good for the complexion," I said as I sat down with a grin.

"Complexion, nothing. I know what's upset her, Lizzie. When she shovelled up the apples there were one or two snails on them. A few wasps too and it's put her off the cider," he leaned back in his chair and laughed heartily. Turning to me he said, "Look here, my gell, all impurities in the cider will all work out when it's in the barrel. You will see a dirty-looking froth coming out of the barrel bung hole. That's the impurities and that's wasps, snails and all, when that's out your barrel is ready for sealing up and after a few weeks you will draw out golden, clear, sparkling cider, so there. Get you on with your cider — you need summat good inside yer, there's work to do." So saying, he picked up the tumbler of water and poured it away down the sink.

Well, I had cider after all. After bait was over I went back to the cider-making and after about an hour Uncle came in to examine the pulp again and declared it good enough to go into the press. The horse was put into the stable while we gathered the pulp up in pails. The press was in the same shed.

It seemed to me like a flat board. On it Uncle laid what seemed to me a sheet of dark brown felt. On this was placed a thick layer of the apple pulp. Another piece of felt was laid on top, making the whole lot look like a sandwich. On top again another thick wad of apple pulp, then another piece of felt. Under the press there was a fifty-gallon butt to catch the dripping juice. The top seemed like the screw of a mangle and as it was turned so it brought another piece of board the size of a four-foot-square table-top down on to the felt.

"That", Uncle explained, "is to help squeeze the juice out."

"How long will that take to drain out, Uncle?"

"Oh, a few days, but we are going to get another lot done to go on top of that and then tomorrow morning I want you to come up and do one more pulping. That should do it, I think."

Aunt Lizzie called out that dinner would be ready in half an hour so Uncle and I got the fruit ready in the stone trough so that we could start after dinner.

"I'll come and give you a hand after dinner. Couldn't this morning, a few jobs to do you know, but after I've given the little pigs their dinner I'll come and follow the old horse round a bit to give you a rest."

Dinner over, we sat a few minutes talking, then Uncle said we would get on with the job. We fixed the horse up and again in answer to my 'Gee up', he trotted round with me following, raking the apples loose as the wheel squashed them flat. Uncle came in about an hour later to say that he would be with me in about five minutes, but when he did come he had barely started following behind the wheel when a friend of his arrived to see him.

"Well, come on, Harry. I expect you can do with a glass of cider!"

Harry said he could; they turned away to the barn, Uncle calling over his shoulder to me, "Shan't be long, gell, carry on, I'll be back in a few minutes," The few minutes spread into an hour. I thought the pulp might be ready now, seeing I had been on the job for two hours. I stopped the horse and went in to Aunt Lizzie.

"Could you come and see this pulp, Aunt Lizzie? I've been doing it now for two hours and Uncle is not here for me to ask him."

"Is he still in the barn? I saw Harry Vaughn come an hour ago. I'll go and shift them. Harry Vaughn is like your uncle, he'd sit and drink until the cider run out of his eyes." So saying, she went into the barn. What she said to the two men I don't know but they were out of there in two minutes. Both men looked as if they had had enough cider. Harry Vaughn went off without a word, down to the yard, through the gate and about his business. "You were supposed to be helping that girl, instead you have messed about all morning, and now you're messing about all afternoon too. You're always the same. Let you find an old crony who will come and help to hold the barrel up and you're happy."

I helped Uncle get the pulp into the 'aires' as he called the felt pieces and very soon I was on my two-mile trek home. I was anxious to get there, the poultry would want feeding, the pigs too. These jobs I got done, and then prepared the evening meal.

Dinner over and the dog fed, Father asked how the day had gone. I told him about Aunt Lizzie scolding Uncle Ted for being in the barn and not giving a hand to make the cider. Father laughed. "Yes," he said as he filled his pipe, "she isn't much size up against him, but he gets away with nothing.

Ted's all right but he is the kind that won't do more than he can help."

Next morning I went to the Headlands Farm again but only for the morning. As I thought, Uncle left me to the cider-making again, after he had fixed the horse to the mill. I saw Aunt Lizzie at bait time, and we had a bit of a chat. It started to rain, as I set out for home, after telling Aunt Lizzie I would see her on the morrow.

"Yes, do that. I wish we had more time to have a long talk together, but that must be when we are not so busy, eh?"

As I walked the rain became heavy. I sheltered under a big oak tree, till the storm eased a little. Then thunder burst, and I decided I had better keep going. The thunder increased in volume, the lightning flashed all round with a vivid purple light. I ran down the long hill towards the village, and did not pause until I got in sight of its first few straggling cottages.

I walked on, and reached the doorway of the village shop, and there I stood to shelter until the storm eased again. Some ten minutes later, when the rain was not so heavy I ran off again, only to find some three hundred yards or so from the shop that for quite a distance the road was like a pond. I decided I could not get much more soaked than I was, so I waded through the water, and some twenty minutes later was at Woodlands. The dog was asleep in his kennel when I arrived, but was soon down and prancing round excitedly, very glad to see me, although he was not as a rule a dog to show affection, and hated being cuddled.

When I had quietened him and after I had taken off my wet coat I went in search of dry clothes. I guessed Father would be home soon, as I knew he could not have worked in the rain, so I lit the fire, and very soon the room felt warm and cosy.

I was quite surprised when Mr Dent, Father's boss, brought him home in his car. I went out to the gate when I heard the car stop, and Mr Dent called out with a laugh, "Bob's chauffeur has brought him home, right to the gate." In one moment with a wave of his hand he drove off. Father explained that Mr Dent went round to where he was working, and told him as he could do nothing in such weather he might just as well go home.

I had placed my wet boots on the fender in front of the fire, hoping that Father would pass some comment on their dilapidated condition. I intended to raise the subject again if he did not. When dinner was over we turned our chairs from the table towards the fire.

Father asked for news about Aunt Lizzie and Uncle Ted. I said there was no news, that I had hardly got there before Uncle had got me started on the cider-making, and that as usual I had been left to get on with it, as he had a lot of jobs to see to. "We got one lot through the mill," I said, "then it was dinner time. After dinner we got it into the press, then I came away."

"I suppose you must go up tomorrow?" Father asked.

"Yes, then I'll have a day at home, and go up again if I'm needed. But I'm worried about my boots; look at them, I can't wear them any more." Father picked one boot off the fender, where it had been drying.

He put it down after turning it round for inspection.

"Hm," he said with a sigh, "I will give you some money in the morning, you had better call into the village shop and get yourself a good strong pair of boots. Something that will stand up to hard wear, and no fancy stuff, mind."

"No, Father," I answered, thankful at last that this boot business was settled.

17

When Father had gone off to work next morning I hurriedly did the housework, fed the poultry, put the cattle out and began to get ready to go out. I was happy for that very morning I was going to buy a new pair of boots. I sang as I dressed.

Bruce was lying in the yard, barking at everyone who passed by the gate. When there was no-one to bark at he sometimes barked at the squirrels that came into the hedge after nuts, or at the birds. But there was a difference in his bark when he barked at people, and I always knew if anyone approached the gate. I was nearly ready to go out, and I stopped to think what I had left undone. I did not want anything to be left that should be done inside. I'd have plenty to do outside with the stock when I came home.

I was just about to leave when I realised by the dog's bark that someone was coming to the house. "Oh dear, I hope it is not Mr Pressley, I shall never get rid of him," I said to myself.

I went to the scullery door to look, and was most surprised to see Paul coming up the yard, Bruce prancing round him as he walked.

"Down dog, down dog," said Paul and I in unison.

"What has brought you, Paul? I don't often get a visit from you," I asked as he followed me into the living room.

"No, and I wouldna' be here now, but I've got some bad news," he said as he sat in the chair.

"What's wrong?" I enquired.

"Mother passed away last night, or early this morning," he replied.

I stood aghast at the news.

"Aunt Lizzie! Dead? I saw her only yesterday," I said.

"Yes, Father told me this morning. You see, Mother has slept for a long time in the little bedroom at the top of the stairs. She was a light sleeper and Father disturbed her as he is restless in bed, so she used to say. Well, they went to bed as usual, she seemed her usual self. But Father woke and found it was half past six and, that being late for them, he called out to Mother that they had overslept. As he got no reply after calling two or three times he got out of bed, and went to her room and found she had passed away. She was quite cold, and he thought she must have died some hours before. He rushed down to the neighbours in that little cottage on the right-hand side, you know the one, you've passed it. Old George Aikens put the horse to the trap and came to tell me he had left Father at his cottage. So of course, I have been up there, and came down to tell you about it. Can you go up?" he asked as he stood up ready to leave.

"Yes, I'll go up this morning. I was due up to help with the cider-making anyway but I guess that's off for the present. Tell me, Paul, was it her heart? I thought she did not look so well yesterday, but she said she was all right."

"Yes, her heart, we all knew that her heart was weak; well, I must go, there's the milking to see to and I know Lil will be all upset, she was very fond of Mother."

Paul departed, and I was on my way to the village in a matter of minutes. As I walked towards the village I thought of Aunt Lizzie. I had seen her in all about half a dozen times, once only to make a visit, the other times I had seen her very briefly when I went up to work. We had never really had time to sit and chat or to have that long talk she had mentioned only the previous day. Now we would never talk together. I had liked her from the very beginning and we could have been real friends. I had never taken to Lil, her remoteness had always kept me back. We could never have been real friends.

I was going to miss Aunt Lizzie, I told myself, the very knowledge that she was there even though I saw her so seldom had warmed my heart.

When I got to the village I decided, in spite of everything, to go into the shop to buy my boots. The short time it would take to get them I thought would make no difference to Aunt Lizzie now. I bore in mind my father's warning. "Get a good strong pair of boots now, no fancy stuff, mind." Well, he was right, one needed a strong pair of boots to stand up to the flooded roads we sometimes had after heavy rains, and to stand the mud and slush of the farm.

When I got to the farm I found Uncle sitting in the chair by the table, with a half-empty jug of cider beside him. I knew him well enough to be able to decide that the jug had been full. It was not his practice to fetch only half a jug from the barrel.

"Well, Uncle?" I said as I went into the kitchen, "I'm very sorry about this." I put my hand on his shoulder. "It's all so sudden, but you must not let it get you down, must you? Do try to remember you've had a good many years together, and this has to happen sometime to us all." I sat in the chair in front of him.

"Yes, gell, we've had a lot of years together, forty-two of them in fact. She was a good 'un if ever there was, an' I don't know how I shall carry on."

"It's a bit soon to decide, Uncle, but perhaps you will go to live with Paul or Edward, and give up this place now. I'm sure they will offer you a corner in their houses."

"Yes, maybe, maybe, but I do not know as I want it. I have bin used to doing as I like in my own home, and I couldna' do as I like in someone else's. No, gell, I can't decide yet, what I'll do. Anyway, they havena' asked me yet, there's been no time. Lil will come up this afternoon with Paul, but they won't stay for long. Paul will have to bring her and the little 'un, and get home in time for the children coming home from school."

I asked where Aunt Lizzie was, and he said in the bedroom at the top of the stairs. He said I could go up. When I asked him to come upstairs with me, he shuddered. "No, gell, I don't want to — you go," he said.

I walked slowly up the stairs and I know not why but the strange feeling I suppose that most people get when entering the presence of a dead person assailed me. I had never gone into a room where a dead person lay before. Aunt Lizzie lay on the bed, covered by a large white sheet. Uncle told me afterwards that the neighbour had done the 'laying out'. White covers had been placed on the dressing table and trunks, that Aunt had covered in her lifetime with cretonne, to hide the fact that they were trunks. The room had little else in furniture. On the table a candle still burned. I gazed at Aunt. Her grey eyes that had twinkled at me yesterday, were now closed. Her rosy cheeks were now pallid. I turned and walked away quietly as if the noise I might make would disturb her sleep.

When I returned to the kitchen Uncle was just coming in through the door with another jug of cider.

"You must not keep on drinking cider, Uncle, there's work to be done, you know dear, life must go on. Besides you are bound to have callers — it won't do for people to see you fuddled; give me that jug now, let me put it away for a while."

I took the jug from his hand, and he made no effort to resist me. "Yes, you be right, gell, the work must be done," and so saying he walked out of the house on to the yard, and presently he went into the cowshed. I did not see him again until I called him for dinner, but I had not looked for him, as I had been busy tidying up the house. I had closed the door between the stairway and the kitchen, I felt better that way.

For a while dinner went on in silence, but presently Uncle said, "I've been thinking, gell, life is just like a candle. When a babby is born a new candle is lit. When you're halfway through life it's half burnt, when you get on to my age, which is sixty-five now, your aunt was two years younger than me, well the old candle gets low, doesn't it?" He put his fork on the plate and sat looking intently at me.

"Why yes, I suppose so, you could look at it that way Uncle, but your candle can burn on for a long time, it's up to you; if you put the candle in a draught — it burns out quicker; if it's away from the draught — it would burn longer. You're not an old man and you could find some happy days yet. For that matter who can say today that they will be alive tomorrow, the scientists can't tell us that, Uncle, and it's up to you and me how we look at things."

"H'm" was his only comment.

After dinner he went off, I guessed to feed the pigs. Presently

Edward's wife arrived. I had not seen her before, and had seen Edward only once. I liked her at once, but judged she was some years older than him. Very soon afterwards I left, and gave a promise to come up next day.

I went as promised next day, but found Lil and Paul there when I arrived. I felt surprised that they were there so early, as it was barely ten o'clock when I arrived but they explained that they had taken the boys to school, and as it was halfway to Headlands, they had gone on as they wanted to talk to Uncle about the future. I did not wish to intrude on what might be a private conversation, and in view of the fact that they intended to remain there until after dinner I just went out to see Uncle for a few minutes to say I would be up the next morning. The funeral he told me, would be at two o'clock the next day.

"Will you go to the funeral, my dear?" he asked. I said I would not as I had nothing suitable to wear, but would go up to stay in the house, and to make a meal ready for when they got back; I added that Father would be at the church when they arrived there.

I was glad to get home, there was much to be done. The dog was pleased to be released from the chain, and the poultry was soon fed and quietened. As I had finished the outside work, and was just about to fill the kettle at the water spout a voice from over the hedge startled me.

"There you are, Elizabeth," Mr Pressley called.

"Oh — oh, how you startled me!" I gasped as I stood up.

"You must have a guilty conscience, my dear, to get startled like that."

I told him sharply that my conscience was all right.

"So's mine, although there's some folk as thinks it isna'," he replied.

"Who would that be, Mr Pressley?" I said as I put the bucket of water on the ground.

"Lots of folk," he snorted. "I don't know where Ada is, or where she went. I've nothing to hide or to fear either." As he spoke his voice rose, until his last words ended almost in a scream.

I tried to calm him down. After a minute or two he said, "You're right, of course, I have nothing to worry about — but I've felt people avoid me, Mrs Jones when I go to see her can never stop to speak like she used to, her's got something to do that won't wait. When I goes to the village to get my pension people stare at me. I knows what they're thinking. That I have harmed Ada. P'raps they think I've killed her. You too, I never see you now — do you avoid me too?"

I tried to tell him that he imagined it all, that people didn't stare. That I had been away so much at Headlands Farm and to Paul's wife each week to help with the butter-making, that I was probably away when he came, at either of these places.

After a few more minutes' conversation I managed to get into the house, and to do the jobs I had to do, but I was worried. I knew I had been inclined to think that Mr Pressley knew more about Ada's disappearance than he had said. I knew too that they had come to blows on more than one occasion. But, I reasoned, she may have got tired of the years of domination, and finally left him. The old man was in need of help, but I was scared for some reason to go up to his house, and to be in the house with him alone.

The morning of the funeral arrived, and Father stayed home from work to attend it. I was going up to Headlands Farm to do what was needed, and intended to leave when the family returned from the funeral. The days were growing short, and it was necessary to feed the pigs and poultry early to avoid them going to bed not properly fed. As it was it would be sixteen hours before they would get their first meal in the morning, after the previous day's feed. I left home soon after nine o'clock. Father would keep himself busy he said, cleaning out a gutter in the top orchard, that was getting clogged with leaves that had been shed into it by the rain.

Edward's wife Polly was at the farm when I arrived. They had come early, not knowing what arrangements had been made. Edward, she said, was somewhere out around the farm with his father. I asked her what arrangements Uncle would be making for his future now he was alone.

"That's what we hope can be settled this afternoon when we all return from the church," she said.

I asked what she would like Uncle to do. She replied, "Well, you see, if he stays here for the present he would put in a notice to his landlord. He doesn't own the place you know, so if he puts his notice in, he would have to stay until February. But he could not look after himself — Mother spoilt him, he couldn't cook for himself. Edward would like to take over the farm, and if that is agreeable to his father we would come to live here, and his father would still be in his own house, and I could look after him.

"I don't know how Paul and Lil would like that, that remains to be seen. He has, no doubt, I mean Father, been having thoughts of his own on the matter. We shall know this afternoon. He has not been sleeping in the house since Mother died — and I do not believe he will ever sleep in the house alone."

I agreed with what she said, and said I hoped things would be settled soon.

The funeral was over and I left the farm, and got home as Father had finished the feeding. He wanted to know if there had been any arrangements about Uncle's future, and I replied that I had left the house when they were all settled to a meal. That they would talk no doubt after I left.

I neither saw nor heard any more until I went to Lil's on my usual Thursday morning job. We talked of various things for a few minutes, and then I brought the conversation round to Uncle Ted. I asked if they had seen him since the funeral.

Lil replied that they had seen him only on the day of the funeral, and that they had asked about his plans. She said he had refused to leave the farm, that he did not want Edward and Polly to come to live there; and as he had three months to go before he could leave he was going to ask Maud Evans who lived in the village to come to housekeep for him. In the meantime until he saw Maud Evans, the neighbour Mrs Aikens would 'do for him'.

There was silence for a while, as I turned the churn. The

cream slopped round as the churn turned. Lil went off into the other room, but returned after a few minutes.

"Lil," I said, "perhaps Uncle does not want to give up farming at all, he may decide he is not yet ready to retire. In that case he must have someone in to look after him and the place."

"I know, and he could have Edward and Polly; Edward could get work at Dent's Farm, Father could run his farm as usual and Polly would care for him. But no, he wants Maudie Evans. He had this all thought out well, by the day of the funeral. Paul is furious about it!"

She turned away, and began to break up some salt to put into the churn.

"Who is Maudie Evans? I have never heard of her before." I stopped turning and waited for Lil to get the salt fine enough.

"She's in her thirties, and she's a widow. About two years ago Paul's mother was ill, and it was necessary to have someone in to do things. Mother was in bed for about a month. Well, she objected to the behaviour of father and Maud Evans, said they were too frivolous, and Maud had to leave. Well now, we are all against it. Oh I tell you, Paul's mad about it." Lil put the salt in through the bung-hole of the churn. The bung was tightly fastened and I began to turn again.

When I got home that evening I told Father Lil's news. He was silent for quite a while. Then he said he would visit Uncle Ted on Sunday.

Sunday morning Father was away in good time and did not return until teatime. I asked him what Uncle had said, and he replied that Maud Evans was going to the farm as housekeeper to Uncle the next day, but later at tea he said, "It would never surprise me if your Uncle does not marry quite soon. In a matter of months I mean, and to Maud Evans. I feel there is some attraction there, though it's an awful thing to say, your Aunt only just been laid to rest. My father did the same thing."

He went on to say that when his mother died, the family being all grown up, and away from home, his father had to have someone to keep house. He had a flourishing business, as a butcher, at the time. The housekeeper was a young and attractive woman.

"In next to no time they were married. Six months later Father died, and his wife had all he left; we his family got nothing. It would never surprise me if your uncle does the same."

18

All through the war years, the church bells had been silent. Now on this frosty November morning as I walked to the village I heard the church bells ringing, all five of them, and I wondered what had happened. I met a couple of people walking towards me.

"What has happened?" I asked.

"The war is over, that's what's happened," one of them said excitedly.

"Are you sure?"

"Yes. There's great excitement in the village. We've won the war. Germany is beaten — oh, thank God for that."

In the village there were more people wandering about and talking and laughing in little groups than I had ever seen before. One old fellow was playing a jig on a violin, one or two dancing — at first self-consciously, then others joining in, laughing and shouting. I wondered if Father had heard the news and hurried home — but on the way I called in to see Mrs Jones.

"This would call for a drink," she said, "but I have nothing stronger than tea. Let's have a cup of tea and a bit of my cake." However, I thought I oughtn't to stay too long in case my father had come home.

My father got back at about four. He came in Mr Dent's car.

"We have all been celebrating the end of the war, Miss Walker," Mr Dent said. "And all the men and myself celebrated for once not with cider but something stronger — several bottles of wine."

After he'd gone, Father sat in his chair, bleary-eyed.

"What a day, what a day," he kept saying, till he fell asleep.

I got busy preparing the dinner, then quickly fed the pigs

and the hens and got the two cattle down from the orchard and fixed them up with hay.

"That'll mean your mother's job will be coming to an end," Father said over dinner.

I agreed that it was possible, and I wondered if, when it did, she would return to my father.

A few days later, we had a letter from my mother. She said they had had a wonderful party in the works canteen and she supposed the munition works would be sacking their employees in a couple of months' time. She added that she was sending a present for my father and me for Christmas.

"I hope she doesn't forget this one," I said. "She promised us a present some time ago and we never got it." The thought of a Christmas present was pleasing — it was many years since I had received a Christmas present from anyone. I smiled wryly at the thought of Christmas presents from Mother. In fact I could only remember having received one since the time when I was about six years old. Father came home from work with a little brown hen in his wood bag. It was a large bag called a 'frail' and made of straw.

It seems the little hen had been found in one of the trucks that had come on to the siding to be refilled with coal. It was probable she had jumped into the truck when it had been stationary, and then found she could not get out. Hens are so stupid, they will manage to poke a hole under the wire netting round their run, but can never find their way back through the same hole. Well, the little hen was given to me, but she must have been a wandering hen for one day we found she was missing. Mother said she must have flown into someone's back yard, and most likely became their dinner.

Father wrote to Mother to say the best Christmas present she could give us both would be for her to take her place at Woodlands. He said we managed very well, but that it would be better if she were there. On this Mother made no comment when next she wrote.

Christmas day dawned. Snow had been falling all night, and when we arose at seven o'clock — an hour later than usual — it was over a foot deep outside the scullery door. Before I could put the kettle on to boil I had to dig through the snow to the water spout.

Later at breakfast Father said, "Your mother's parcel did not arrive after all."

"There's an old saying, Father, that he who expects nothing shall not be disappointed. I learnt that long ago, at least as regards Christmas presents. No, I hadn't expected a present, but the post does come today, we may get a parcel yet."

Breakfast over, Father proceeded to dig pathways through the snow to the gate, the cowshed, the barns and the poultry houses. When I had cleared the table I joined him. And after the feeding was done, and the cattle and pigs bedded down with plenty of straw, Father brought in some logs and banked up the fire.

"I ain't going very far from the fire today, except to feed the stock. That's the worst o' farming, it's a seven-day-a-week job, and holidays make no difference."

I agreed.

Presently, as I stood by the window looking up the road, I saw the postman come zigzagging down it.

"The postman is coming," I said. "I should say the road is pretty bad, the way he's wobbling about." Father came to the window.

"Hm, he must have got quite a load on his back. Yes, poor devil, it isn't funny for them, is it? We all think we have got all the troubles until we see or hear someone else's."

He seemed to be slowing down, and Father went to the yard door to see if he was going to stop. He did, and I heard Father's voice, "I bet the roads are bad this morning, Gillum."

"So they are, so they are. Worse in some places than others. Not so bad down here now 'cos there's been some traffic down here. The worst part is people ain't got much sense. You'd think now they would clear the snow away from their gates? How the 'ell do they expect me to deliver letters when the gate is bunged up with snow?"

"Yes, I can see what you mean. What do you do when you can't open the gates?" Father asked.

"Oh, shout like 'ell and make them come and get their

letters and parcels if they want'm. I just stands by the gate. You should see some on 'um when I go to the door some-times. Some shoves an arm round the door, some opens the door. There they are, hair in curlers, face not washed. Fair put you off, it does."

Both men were laughing, as I carried a hot cup of tea down to the gate.

"Thought you'd like a hot drink, Mr Gillum, to warm your tummy up. Father could offer you cider — we have nothing stronger, but I thought tea would be better." Gillum laughed.

"I'm being posh today, I've had sherry, port and a whisky —so I guess a cup of tea will help make a good mixture. I'll have the cider another day." I could see he was not too sober, and by the size of the bag on his back he had quite a lot to deliver. I guessed he would be pretty tipsy by the time he had finished.

I took the parcel out of Father's hands, and after wishing the postman a happy Christmas, I walked up to the house.

The parcel was a small one, and it was soon opened. It contained a box of crackers, a pair of hand-knitted socks for Father, and a small box for me which I eagerly opened. The contents made me laugh, and laugh, and then I cried. The box contained a pair of elastic garters, prettily covered with ribbon, with a doll's head, very tiny on what was supposed to be the front.

Father came in, and was surprised to see my tears. "Why the tears?" he asked.

"I suppose I'm disappointed. Oh, I know I shouldn't be," I said as I mopped my eyes, "but I had expected something different."

"Well, what did you expect, did you send your mother anything?"

"Father, how could I? I had no money. Oh, these are pretty, but I don't wear garters."

I put the garters back into the box. Father was busy turning his socks over. He was pleased with them. Later on, I felt different about my present. After all, I reflected, Mother had thought them nice, and I felt sorry to have been so ungrateful. I even put them on, although they were not a necessary item.

When dinner was ready we sat down at the table to eat, and by the time the pudding was consumed I felt quite happy. I remembered the crackers. "Pull, Father," I said as I took one from the box. Father pulled, and in the half he had there was a motto, 'Don't put off for tomorrow, what you can do today', also a child's whistle. "Now mine, Father." The cracker was pulled and a slip of paper fell on to the floor. It read, 'Look forward to tomorrow'.

We turned our chairs to the blazing fire, and Father was soon fast asleep. I sat and stared at the fire. I thought of my Christmas with the Armstrongs. What fun we had had, the children with their stockings at the foot of the bed crammed with toys. How excited they had been. I got up quietly and walked outside. It had started to rain.

The snow will soon be washed away, I thought. I looked all round at the trees bare of leaf. The snow had fallen off them already, and they looked like war-torn warriors. In the distance I could see the smoke just barely rising from the chimneys of one of the cottages down the road. All around was silence, and I felt depressed and lonely. Not for me the country, with its green foliage, or the empty, silent leafless trees. I liked rows of houses, with smoke issuing from the chimneys; they spoke of life. I liked the shop windows, brilliantly lit; even if they had things in them I could not afford to buy I loved to see them just the same. I loved to see people walking in the streets, people who passed about their own business. To me the country was a lonely place, made more lonely by my father who wished to keep unto himself, and to keep me that way too.

There and then I told myself that soon, very soon, when Father would be at work I would walk right into Leominster, just to see the shops.

19

The snow of Christmas Day disappeared, only to be followed a few days later with more heavy snow. It snowed on and off for days. Paths we made to the cowshed and poultry houses were soon filled in again. Each day we made new paths, then heavy rain made the flat country flooded, and we who lived on Dilwyn Common had to wade through water often up to our thighs to get to the village for supplies. The worst was yet to come.

It was about a fortnight after the floods had gone down, and we had had about four days of dry weather. Then one Saturday afternoon it was very cold, and the water in the rainwater butt had frozen. Then it began to rain gently, and as the rain fell so it froze. Very soon the ground was covered with a sheet of ice, and by the look of the sky the rain was going to continue.

Father and I went out to feed the stock and, when we had finished, our hats were fringed with little icicles. I did not venture outside again after we had locked up the animals. Foxes roamed the ground at night. I could hear the vixen calling to her mate. She made a most weird noise, I can only liken it to the sound of someone being strangled.

Back in the autumn I remember Father and I had been woken one night by a sort of banging noise in the orchard. There was no doubt at all that the sound came from outside the small poultry house, not far from the gate. I called to Father that I believed a fox was worrying the poultry, and was out of bed in a second, and picking up the torch off the bedside table I dashed out of the house and up the cobble-stoned path, through the gate and into the orchard. Father quickly followed, just in time to see a fox carrying off one of the hens. I could not get at him, but I flung the torch. It landed about a foot in front of him. The shock made him drop the fowl, and he scampered away. I picked up the fowl, and then we discovered four others on their backs on the ground. The birds inside the house were making a lot of noise. We had found that the shutter or 'pop hole' of the house had not been fastened at locking-up time. The five birds were practically dead and, on examination next day, they had been quite inedible.

Next morning the ice was considerably thicker. It must have rained and frozen a good part of the night.

"Be careful how you go," said Father as I stepped out over the doorstep. I had gone just two or three steps outside when I fell. After I had recovered myself, I got up and took two or three more steps, and down I went again.

"It's no good, Father, you can't walk on it," I said.

"Well, come inside a minute, we'll have to think what we can do. It's a devil, isn't it? Did you hurt yourself?" he asked.

"Yes, I bet I shan't be able to sit down in comfort for a week or two," I said as I rubbed my sore places. Father said that if we put old socks over our shoes maybe it would help to grip on the ground, but he fell just the same, and I decided that it would be better for me to crawl, that I could not fall that way. I did so, and managed to find the poultry. They would not come out of their houses, so I placed food and water as near the houses as I could and left them to it.

Next day the ground was still frozen hard.

The bad weather made Father very irritable, as he could not go to work and couldn't get his tobacco. He had been at home for about a month owing to the weather, and the thought that Mr Dent his boss would not have much for him to do. The long dark evenings with nothing to do worried us both. The only reading material we had were the newspapers delivered on Sundays and the books lent to me by the shopkeeper's wife.

I had used up silk cottons that I brought to Dilwyn with me long ago, so I had no sewing to do, and I was glad when bedtime came, so we could go to sleep and awake to the next morning with work to do.

During these weeks that Father was at home he never left the house, even to go and see his brother. That he missed my mother I knew, in the little things he said. He told me of their courting days; he had met her on a farm. They had both worked for the same farmer, and he would say how smart she had been, with a tiny eighteen-inch waist, and her 'mop of lovely red hair'. We were both unhappy, although we hid the thoughts we had from each other.

He wanted Mother; I wanted to go where I could work and earn money, to replace my stock of clothes, and to own a few shillings to have to spend. But not for one moment would I have considered saying I wanted to leave. I was there until such times as Mother would decide to come to him, as come she would, I felt sure. When she did, Mother would alter a lot of things or pack up and go again.

During the time Father had been home, I had seen nothing of Mrs Jones.

Mr Pressley had walked up the road several times, and I had seen him from the kitchen window. He glanced occasionally towards the house, but he never came to the gate. I thought he had seen Father round the place, and as Father was always very curt to him he would not call. But I had seen him through the gap in the hedge. He seemed cleaner but he still wore the old dark blanket wrapped round him like a skirt.

I had seen, too, a middle-aged woman, at the house. On one occasion she was busy shaking out the mats, and I thought maybe it could be his daughter-in-law who came to clean for him. I had heard his son lived only a few miles away.

I often wondered about Ada. I wondered whether she had been found, but there was no way of getting any news.

At last the weather improved and, although the sun shone sickly through the clouds, one was grateful. There had been so many cloudy, misty days and what little sun we saw at least made my heart rejoice. True, the weather was cold, but it was dry, and the snowdrops that grew by the cobble-stoned path were a fine show. I marvelled they could grow through such bad weather, rearing their little heads through the snow and ice we had had. Father returned to work, and I believe he was glad to go.

On the third day that he went to work I decided that at last the day had come for me to walk into Leominster. True I had not a penny to my name, but that did not worry me — I was going to see the shops. I saw to all the feeding, the cattle had not been out for weeks in the orchard, during the bad weather, but were allowed out on the yard for a short spell when weather permitted.

I let them out for about twenty minutes, then drove them back into the cowshed.

"Tomorrow, if it's nice, you shall go into the orchard maybe, but not today, I'm going out," I told them, as I fastened them up.

I polished my boots — they were more suitable for walking — and very soon I was on my way. The day was cold but bright, and I set off at a good pace and reached Leominster at about eleven o'clock.

I wandered round looking at the shop windows. The materials and dresses all thrilled me. Shoe shops, too. I thought of my 'best' pair of shoes, I wore them but seldom, and they were not at their best, I told myself. There were plenty in the window that I liked but I did not in any way worry that I could not buy.

Toy shops fascinated me, the dolls particularly. I remembered the doll my father had bought me once. I could be about five or six years old. I would not let the shop man pack it up, and I carried it so carefully. But when we got on the train to come home I suppose I must have been very tired, and somehow it was left on the seat of the carriage. Mother and Father, busy picking up their parcels after shopping and hustling a very sleepy child on to the platform, probably thought I had it. When the train started off out of the station, I realised my loss, and set up such a roar, but it was too late, my doll had gone off with the train.

After I had seen enough of the shops I turned towards home, and as Dilwyn church struck two I was but a few yards from home. I had left the key of the house under a pail, on the old cider wheel.

When I reached the gate, looking into the yard I could see the door was open, and looking up to the chimney I saw there was smoke issuing from it. I stood shocked to a standstill. Father was home, why was he home at two o'clock? I pushed the gate open and walked slowly up to the house through the open door, and into the scullery, crossed the scullery and looked through the doorway into the kitchen. Father was sitting by the fire. He looked up.

"Where have you been?" he said, quietly.

"To Leominster to see the shops," I said in like tones.

"To Leominster to see the shops? God in Heaven, why?"

"You wouldn't understand, Father, but I promised myself the walk a little while ago — there was no other way for me to get there but walk, so I walked."

"Why didn't you say you were going this morning?" he asked as he rose from his chair.

"Because you would not have let me go," I replied, standing by the table.

"Did you go to buy anything?"

"No. I had no money. I just went because I wanted to see the shops, that's all."

"So you walked twelve miles, back and fore, just to see the shops, and I come home to find you out and no fire in the grate, and you off galavanting."

"I have been off from here for four hours, several times, when I've been off to Uncle Ted's, to make cider — to go for once for myself for four hours should not matter very much," I said as I took my coat off. He advanced quickly towards me, and stood towering in front of me with his fist clenched.

"For two pins I'd knock you down," he shouted at me.

I looked up at his raised fist. I could not believe that my father could threaten to knock me down, and I stared at him.

"Get some dinner," he shouted. Dinner was prepared, and eaten in silence, at least what was eaten for we both left the table with it hardly touched. I had come home starving after my twelve-mile walk, but now what little I had eaten nearly choked me, and I gave up the attempt.

How I longed to get away! But matters were to come to a head a few weeks later.

My father was always asking me to go to the village shop to get him supplies of tobacco. And I frequently had trouble getting it. Sometimes there was none, and sometimes the shopkeeper would ration it to half an ounce a customer. Sometimes Father had no tobacco in the house at all and those were days when I needed to be very careful, as he was inclined to be very short-tempered then.

The day the trouble happened was a wet day and I was told to go to the village to see if the tobacco had come in. My father was digging a ditch in the lower part of the meadow, as the water had collected up with the last snows and the rain, and normally when he worked he liked to chew his tobacco.

Before I left the house I put some wood on the fire, but I had no coal, and I set off in the rain. I did not possess an umbrella. I walked the mile and a half to the village to be told yet again that the tobacco had not come in, and when I got back to the house, I could see that my father was in by the light in the window. He was taking off his sodden coat, as I stood dripping in the doorway.

"Did you let the fire go out? You knew I would be wet when I came in," he shouted. "Where's my tobacco?"

"I've just walked three miles to the village and back. The tobacco hasn't come in yet. You can't expect a wood fire to keep burning for that length of time. I'm sorry. There's some dry kindling wood in the barn. I'll get it going again soon."

It was already getting dark and I took a box of matches out with me to the barn. My father stood lowering in the doorway.

"You'll set the barn on fire with those matches," he said.

"It's only one match," I said. "I've got the wood now. The match is safely out."

He raised his arm with his fist clenched. "I've a good mind to knock you down."

I stared at him. "Don't you hit me. I've done nothing

wrong. It's not my fault the fire went out, and I'm not a child. If you hit me, I promise I'll go to the police house and report you."

He lowered his fist and turned his back on me and walked away to the house. I followed him with the wood.

After I had raked up the dead ash and remade the fire, I took my wet things off and hung them behind the kitchen door.

My father was sitting down now.

"Look you can go, you don't want to be here. Just go, go tonight if you want," he said, his voice rising as he glared at me.

I looked at him steadily. "I will go — tomorrow." And with that I turned my back on him and went into the scullery to prepare the vegetables.

Later we sat by the fire, not speaking. After I had washed the dishes I said I was going to bed and left the room.

I lay in the darkness. I thought he might be calmer in the morning and would try to make amends, although I could not imagine my father apologising. If he was nicer in the morning, I would stay.

In the morning I went down to get the fire going, wash myself in the scullery and prepare the breakfast. I boiled the kettle, made the tea and got out the frying pan, while he was washing in the scullery. Over breakfast we both said not a word to each other.

He got up from his chair.

"Put my food in the bag. I'm going to work," he said.

I did so. He picked the bag up and walked out of the kitchen without another word.

I watched him as he walked up the road, then sat down to think what I should do. I could not go to my mother, who was in Coventry. I could not go to Mrs Armstrong, who would have got someone else by now. There was only my sister in Maesteg.

Well, I thought, she might be willing for me to go to her. She had a shop and was a maternity nurse. Her husband served in the shop, for my sister Rachel did not care for it, and only went in to serve if Charlie (my brother-in-law) had more than two or three customers at a time. My niece, Annie, had just left school so she was maid-of-all-work, but I guessed Rachel would be glad to let me help while I was looking for a job.

I decided to go to my sister. Yes, I would go. I would leave my father. I had wanted to go for a long time. I would not have left him, but now this upset had come. 'I will go,' I told myself.

When I had decided, I stood up, tidied up the house, fed the stock and the dog, boiled the kettle and washed the dishes, peeled the vegetables and put them in a saucepan of cold water, brought the wood indoors and laid it in the fender.

My trunk was only a small one. My father had bought it for me when I had first gone away to work in service. It was a tin trunk enamelled blue inside, and the outside was painted to look like wood. I thought, if I pack that tightly, maybe I can do without the parcel I would have to take plus my small portmanteau. I set to work and managed to get the trunk and portmanteau packed.

I decided that I would borrow two pounds from my father's money upstairs. I felt sure that since my father had threatened to hit me twice, the third time he would carry out his threat.

I put on my hat and coat, locked the back door of our house and walked up the road to Mr Williams's house.

"Mr Williams," I said when he answered the door to my knock. "Could you take me in to the station this morning? I am going by train to my sister."

"Well," he said, leaning on the porch railing. "I suppose I could. If you be prepared to pay me."

"Well, of course, Mr Williams. I would not ask you if I couldn't, now, would I?" I said, laughing.

"All right. What time to you want to go?" he said.

"How soon can you come up to my father's house?"

"Oh, perhaps in twenty minutes to half an hour," said Mr Williams.

And so it was I left Dilwyn and my father's house.

20

My sister Rachel was greatly surprised to see me walk into her shop carrying my portmanteau and, as soon as she had served the customer and seen her depart, she asked why I had come, what about Father and so on.

She turned to go into the living room and I followed, putting my case down in the hall outside the shop. I told her I had left Father and had come to her. I wanted to find a job as soon as possible. Could she put me up? I would help her in the house for my keep but I wanted a job as soon as possible.

"But you don't need to take a job, there is plenty of work here. We have two stalls in the market every Friday and Saturday. We will be glad to have you here," said my sister.

I collected my trunk from the station. I knew that if I stayed with my sister I would be no more than an unpaid servant. I had spent intervals with her before and this had happened to me. I had worked for my keep but now I wanted to take a post as children's nurse and to earn.

I wrote to my father and told him where I was, that I would repay the two pounds as soon as I could, and what I intended to do. I learned afterwards that he wasted no time in writing to my mother telling her I had left him and asking her to come back to him, which she did do as soon as she was free of her commitments in Coventry. As the war was now over all government factories and whatever government works there had been established for the War Effort were ordered to dispense with all unnecessary staff as soon as possible.

So my mother went to see about the furniture she had put in store with friends, and had it at last transferred to Woodlands and settled down with him.

She increased the quantity of poultry. My father allowed her a large poultry house, to be built in the small meadow. She paid for all poultry foods and any cash from poultry sales was her own pocket money. All farmers' wives kept the poultry and profits as their own pin-money, and so did my mother.

I believe she and my father, apart from the odd difference of opinion, were very happy. She must have been a while, however, before going to my father and he had to manage as best he could. Knowing how unused my father was to looking after himself, he must have been very relieved when Mother at last came.

In the meantime, here I was with my sister who was as anxious to keep me with her as I was to get away into a job. Until I could find one I worked hard along with my niece.

It seemed my sister and brother-in-law had taken to making their own mineral waters. They had installed a machine for putting gas into the bottled water, after the different flavoured syrups had been added. So many jets into each bottle. Then the bottles were sealed with screw corks and labelled. Annie would deliver these bottles, in wooden cases, by horse and cart.

The horse, a nice little brown mare with a white streak down its head and nose, worked well and Annie loved her and looked after her well. Annie was a good girl and worked very hard. I remember we made, one morning, twenty dozen pint-bottles of drinks: lemonade, lime juice, sarsaparilla and others. Annie had delivered them out to the various shops who had ordered them. I could well see that my sister could do with me as another pair of hands, but I made it plain that I wanted a post as children's nurse and intended to go as soon as I found such a position.

One day when I was serving a customer in the shop, we were talking and I mentioned I was looking for work as a children's nurse.

"My daughter is working for a nice family," she said. "Mr Walters, that's my daughter's boss, is a very well-known photographer and he has a shop in town, also another place in Bridgend. He does very well. His wife manages the shop at

Bridgend so they need a new nurse. There are two little boys to look after. The other nurse left for some reason and I do know they need someone for the children. My daughter is cook general."

I was very interested and getting the Walters's address, I went that evening to see Mrs Walters. As both Mrs Walters and her husband were there I was pleased to meet my future employers.

I was taken up to the nursery to see the children: Joseph who was just two, and Ivor, aged four.

After some talk, I was engaged for thirty shillings per month, full board and laundry paid for. I arranged to go in two days' time.

I went back to my sister highly delighted. While my sister said she was pleased for me, she and my brother-in-law were disappointed I could not consent to stay with them.

So, I moved in. I had ironed my uniform which had been packed away in my trunk and not touched since I left Mrs Armstrong's.

When I arrived at the Walters's house I was shown upstairs to the night nurseries and was allowed to use a large cupboard to stow away my cases and other belongings. I was given a key to lock up the cupboard so that the children would not interfere with my things. Next I was shown a sizeable dressing table with drawers into which I could put anything else I wished.

I was to sleep in the night nursery with the oldest boy. Little Joseph slept in a cot in his mother's room.

I settled in quite happily. I was shown where the children's clothes were kept, in a large cupboard which was outside on the landing. Ivor always wore white velvet trousers and jackets with little blouses in blue, green or orange, and little Joseph wore blue velvet suits with little frilly blouses or light woollen jumpers. Each child had a completely clean outfit, underwear included, each day, so there was plenty of washing and pressing to do for the children.

All meals for the children and myself were eaten in the day nursery and before Mrs Walters departed to catch the train to Bridgend she kissed the children and gave them each a sweet, just one, out of a bottle. They never asked for more than one sweet, but after tea, I was told to give them another sweet. They never had money given them to spend.

All work was done in the nurseries and, having washed and dressed the children, I was ready to take them out at ten o'clock each morning, bringing them home at twelve-thirty for dinner. Then they were to rest in their cots for one hour, but they were more trouble than the worth of it because they played in their cots or would keep calling to ask if they could get up. When they did get up again they were washed and dressed and taken out, weather permitting. If wet, they played in the day nursery.

I saw little really of Jessie, the other maid, until evening when the children were abed and asleep. I could then go into the kitchen to do the day's washing and ironing and sit with Jessie when her work for the evening was finished. We would sit and chat. I liked Jessie. She was about twenty-eight or so and she said she was not even courting. I was nearly nineteen and, of course, had no boyfriend either, but I could not believe that a nice girl like Jessie should have no boyfriend. She was fair with blue eyes, tall and not too plump. People did not study slimming in those days. They just ate what they felt they needed, with a little of what they fancied if they could get it. No one talked of slimming and diets and slimming pills as one does now. She was a nice girl, nice-looking. She told me she had had one boyfriend, they had courted for two years and then they had parted about three years before — he had a very possessive mother.

I said I was sorry things had turned out that way, and I was truly sorry. We talked a lot in the evenings when we were able to be together. We were happy and I liked the children and my employers.

The children were never easy to get to bed. After tea I would bathe them and at six-thirty put them to bed. They would, however, be naughty and not go to sleep. It usually meant my going upstairs two or three times from the kitchen in answer to their calls, before I could make them settle down. If their mother or father were at home, which was mostly at weekends, they were made to settle down without much trouble. Their mother or dad would threaten a 'smacking' if they did not settle down. But the parents usually arrived after the children had gone to bed as there was developing of pictures that had been taken, and preparation ready for collection or delivery of their work, which kept them busy after their premises were closed. Often they would get a meal before coming home, especially on Jessie's evening off-duty. So the children saw little of their parents, except in the mornings before they left for work and at weekends. Then the children would come in for a lot of indulgence from their mother and father because they saw so little of them.

Life went on and I was happy. Then my sister began to be difficult.

"Why do you want to stay there?"

"Because I'm happy, of course," I said.

"But we could do with you here," said my brother-in-law.

"How long have you been there now? About four months, isn't it?" said my sister.

"Yes, four months and I don't intend to leave," said I. "I am earning. My pay is not large but I am able to buy new clothes and I am happy. I do not want to leave."

And so the matter was closed for the time being. I got to dislike going to their house. I could see they wanted me to work for them for just my keep and I did not want to. My sister's temper often made things unhappy there and quarrels that sometimes happened between my sister and her husband, which often involved Annie, worried me. I was grateful to them for putting me up when I had left my father, but in return, I had worked hard, between housework, shop-serving, helping on the sweet stalls in the market, and making the mineral drinks with Annie. I felt I had done enough to pay for my food and shelter those few weeks I had been there. So I continued with my job, hoping to be left alone, and no more was said.

Then one day, the mistress asked me to call at the ironmonger's shop in the town and ask them to send up some taps suitable for the bathroom basins and baths. They were to be sent up to the house and Mr Walters would select the ones he considered suitable and give them the job of getting the taps fixed. The shop assistant said they did not usually do this sending taps up for selection, but maybe the vanman would bring some up next day seeing the shop would get the job of fixing them.

The taps were brought next day and I spoke to the vanman who was about twenty-five years old and not married, he assured me. He wanted to know if he could meet me when I was off-duty next time.

I did not see him again for about two weeks. I had told him when he asked me to meet him that I would think about it and would tell him next time I met him. When I met him a second time, in the course of taking the children out — Joseph in his pram and Ivor walking beside me — I agreed to go walking with him.

It was May again. The days were long and we walked and talked, along the canal banks, watching the boats pass by. We never held hands, we never kissed goodnight, we were not sweethearts. It was a queer 'do'. When we met we said 'Hello', we never kissed on meeting. I was not in love with him, nor at any time did I think I was. He was just someone to go out with and to have an excuse not to be at my sister's house so often.

Our walks were always in the evening for I was never off-duty until six-thirty and I had to be indoors at my job again at ten-thirty. But those summer evenings I met him were pleasant and he made no passes at me. Men did not do so in those days. They did not take advantage of a girl who gave them no encouragement and I felt quite safe in his company.

But then came a time when I got tired of the long walks with him. My sister asked me where we went one day and I told her, 'just for walks'.

"Does he ever buy you chocolates? Does he ever take you to the pictures?"

"No," I said. "We just go for walks."

"He's a mean boyfriend, isn't he?"

"He's not a sweetheart, if that's what you mean. We're just good friends," I said.

And then, somehow, I saw him in a different light and after consideration I thought, as I went to bed, 'Yes, he is mean. He just takes me walking and a lot of shoe leather I wear out doing it.' And I got to dislike him. After one more walk I told him, when he saw me back to the house, that I would not be going out with him any more.

"Why?" he asked.

"Well, we are only friends, aren't we? I owe you nothing. So I'm just saying we won't go out together again, that's all. Goodnight."

I saw him often after that. We said 'Hello' and went about our business.

2I

When I was twelve years old, nearly thirteen, a boy came to live in a house on the other side of our street in Abercynon. His name was David Broome. He was eighteen months older than I and had already started work in the mine. He played in the street with us, at least he joined the other boys and girls and me, round the street lamp-post to talk.

He ran races with us down the street. He beat us all at running down the street to Mrs Bethel's shop. By the time we got to the shop he was half-way back to the starting-point and when we got back to the lamp-post which was his side of the street, opposite my mother's house, he would be leaning against it laughing as we reached him.

I quarrelled with my friend Margret Walsh over him. I said he was my boyfriend but she claimed him because she had spoken to him over the fence down the garden before I had ever spoken to him. When I was thirteen we were kid sweethearts and, young as I was, still in school, I think I loved him and he me. Margret Walsh knew she was nowhere in the running for David Broome.

His mother and dad were very nice to me and I was sometimes invited into their house for tea. His brother, Thomas, scowled at me and showed he didn't like me but I was told to take no notice. Anyway, Thomas was not always there.

I left school and got a little job for half-a-crown a week, and to earn it I walked for twenty minutes to reach the house where I worked. I had to be there at nine o'clock in the morning and I left at six-thirty. I did not work Saturday afternoons or Sunday. This all happened before I went into service in Penarth, and when my father was still working as traffic manager at the coal mine — on the surface.

Sometimes I went walking with David and his mum and dad and I loved them all, David especially.

Time went by and David went into the army, in the Welsh Regiment, after putting his age as eighteen when he was only sixteen and a half.

I went to Penarth to my first real job. We wrote to each other but when he was sent out to France, his letters became infrequent and we lost each other along the way.

But I never forgot him and, he told me much later, he had never forgotten me.

Up to the time with Mrs Walters I had not seen him for about four years.

One day, my sister visited my mistress, Mrs Walters. I was surprised to see her come to the house and as soon as she departed I went to the lounge door and tapped upon it.

"Come in," came the reply.

"Madam, my sister has just left. I am very interested to know why. I feel it is something that concerns me."

"It is, indeed. I was myself coming to find you," said Mrs Walters.

"Will you tell me, madam, what my sister came about, although I can have a guess myself."

"Yes," said Mrs Walters. "She wishes you to leave here. She says you could stay with her. She has offered you a permanent home and there is no need for you to be in service here or anywhere else."

"My sister is twelve years older than I. I am the youngest of the family but I am now nineteen. I came to my sister to look for a job and I gave her to understand then that I did not want to stay with her; only until I could find work and she agreed to this. I helped with the work of the house and shop for my keep, until such time as I got fixed up. I was with my sister for three weeks before I came here; I have been very happy here and I am fond of the children. I do not think you have had cause to complain. Each time I go to my sister's house when I am off-duty she asks me why I don't leave here and go to her. I know there is so much work to do there, she has a thriving business, but she would not pay me. She would consider a home, with the odd shilling or so to go to the pictures now and again, or a dress not too often and that would be the limit. I will not go there to live. But will you tell me please, what you said to my sister?"

"Yes, I told her I would find out how you felt about this. I thought maybe you had complained about your work here to her," said Mrs Walters. "How do you feel about this job?"

"I have told you, madam, I am happy here. Do I suit you?"

"Of course."

"Then," I said, "I will see my sister tomorrow evening when I am off-duty and I will get this settled once and for all. If I wanted or do want to leave here, I will come to you myself, madam, and no one needs to speak for me," I said.

"Very well," said Mrs Walters. "I don't want to lose you and if either you or I want to part company, we will tell each other. Is that all right?"

"Yes, thank you madam," I said.

I was impatient for the next night to come and as soon as I was free, I changed my uniform — print dress, apron and cap — and was quickly dressed in my own off-duty clothes. Then I was away down to my sister's house.

Hot words were said by both, with my brother-in-law chiming in on my sister's side. I was told I was ungrateful. Hadn't she taken me in when I had nowhere else to go? Surely all she was offering me was a home? I said yes, she was, as an unpaid servant, like her own daughter. "What do you give her for carrying the bulk of the work of this house? If you didn't have her it would cost you a decent weekly wage for another girl. What do you give her? A shilling to go to the pictures once a week. She couldn't leave you because she doesn't own a penny and she has nowhere to go."

I said a lot more and so did my sister and I got up to walk out, but, before I left I told her I had made my own arrangements with Mrs Walters that when I wanted to leave or she wanted me to leave I would have a month's notice in which time I would get myself fixed up. I would not be coming to her again.

I left the house, and them, and did not go there for a long

time. Sometimes, when I was out with the children, I met my sister, but I made no arrangements to call there again.

My mother was settled with my father at Woodlands and I wrote home every week or two. My mother answered my letters when I wrote, did not refer to my father much, or send his love, but I was not over-worried, my mother knew my father very well.

My brothers, all three of them, had been in the army. During the war two of them went overseas. Frank, my eldest brother, had been wounded in the leg, which was to trouble him into old age. He was discharged from the army on a small pension. Jim, too, ended up on a discharge with very bad lungs which in later life were aggravated by too much smoking. All three boys married and had families.

I had seen little of them for years, but had heard of them from my mother. It seemed they were all back in the mines, working underground and not doing too badly. I felt it was the last thing Jim should have done but I could not see what other work he could do. He had been in the mines since he left school.

Then, one day, I got a surprise letter from David Broome. He said he had got my address from my brother John who had obtained it from my mother, as I never wrote to John or the others either.

In his letter to me David said that he was now out of the army — discharged before the war ended — and was living at home with his people. He had lost a leg, above the knee, and had been gassed and shrapnel-wounded from the back of his neck to his waist. He had been supplied with two artificial legs; one to keep in case of accident to the other and he could send the leg when out of order to Roehampton for repairs.

He had been in hospital quite a long time. His leg had been blown off below the knee, but there had been three operations which meant taking more off the leg each time. Now the leg was off above the knee but he was getting along fine with the artificial one and he was looking forward to going to work.

He had been given a hundred per cent pension which was twenty-five shillings per week for life: but he had to get more than that, and intended to apply to the coal mine authorities who had promised employment to all returning miners who wanted their jobs back in the mine after army service.

He would like to hear from me and he gave me his new address, his parents having moved house for one nearer to David's sister and brother. David's other two brothers and sister also lived quite near.

So it seemed that David's family had taken up where they left off and were united again. His parents were well.

I wrote to him as soon as I had time that evening, telling him how pleased I was to hear from him after such a long time and sorry that somehow I never seemed to get his letters when he was away and that was why I had slowly given up writing to him. I was very sorry he had been so badly wounded and was glad he was making the best of things. I hoped he would write to me again.

When I had finished the letter I had to post it that evening. I could not wait until morning when I went out with the children. All that night I lay unable to sleep, thinking of him and the loss of his leg; his wounds on his back and the gas that had affected his lungs. He had lost his leg when he was just eighteen, after being in the army for eighteen months and overseas for just over a year.

I wondered what changes there would be in him, what the war had done to him. I remembered that his family were all athletes. The boys and their father had won cups for running, swimming, boxing and cycling. They were all all-round athletes; what would it do to David, I wondered.

I remembered David telling me that his brother, Thomas, had taught him to swim the hard way. He had taken David into the middle of the River Taff and said, "Now you b . . . , swim to the bank."

"I was scared," said David. "I was eight years old and I had never been in the river, beyond just the edge, up to my thighs at most. There I was, right in the middle of the river and it looked much wider than it was, but I had noticed how Tom had used his legs and arms and I tried. Somehow I got to the bank on my own without too much trouble and I was so pleased with myself that I jumped into the water and swam back into the centre. From that time forward I couldn't be kept out of the river. One day, I was down by the canal and couldn't resist stripping off and going in to swim. I swallowed some water which was far from clean and I ended up by being very ill with diphtheria and nearly died."

Thomas also taught David how to box. He would take him up to the spare bedroom, lock the door to keep their mother out and then, giving David a pair of boxing-gloves, bid him put them on. Then Thomas would get down on to his knees and say, "Come on. Hit me. Come on." And with his gloved hand would sharply bring his fist into David's face.

David said, "I would get mad, and would lash out, but of course, every blow I tried to land, Thomas always parried and it mostly landed on his arms. When I got better I sometimes landed a good right on his face. Then Thomas would get mad and really rough. I would bawl 'Mum, Mum' and my mother would come to the locked door and yell at Thomas. She was sure he was killing me but the lessons went on!"

David used to tell me that his two sisters and his three brothers, himself and his parents all went out cycling at the weekend, every weekend, so long as it was dry and there was no snow. No wonder they were what they were, with such an upbringing.

As I have said, I was very fond of Mr and Mrs Broome. Mrs Broome had a wonderful collection of earrings, all for pierced ears — her ears were pierced many years before. I was only around thirteen years old but how I wanted to have my ears pierced, especially as Mrs Broome said I could have any pair of earrings I liked and could always change them for any other pair I liked. My wish to wear those lovely earrings overcame my common-sense and, when Mr Broome said he could bore my ears for me, when I asked him how, he said, "Oh, a darning needle from the front of the ear and a lump of soap at the back and when the needle goes through the ear it will go into the soap. Quite easy, I assure you." I remember I consented; and soon I was sitting on the chair, my hair pinned back from my ears, and there was Mr Broome endeavouring to get the point of the darning needle through the lobe of my ear. After trying several times without success and the uncomfortable pricking of the needle, we at last decided to leave well alone.

A good job, too, as my father would have whopped me good and hard if I had gone home with earrings in my ears. He was always on about 'the vanity of women' and the 'sinfulness' of it all. Father never said anything about the vanity of men! Even now, I shudder to think how my father would have acted. Absolute obedience was the keyword to his life. My father did not have to tell you to behave, he just fixed his eyes on you and you were 'squashed' completely. My brothers were often in trouble over little things — nothing bad, they didn't dare — and their behinds frequently felt the toe of Father's boot.

Now, I had had a letter from David, home from the war, and I had written back.

In a few days' time I had another letter: David said he would like to see me. Could I get a day off to go to see him? His parents sent their love, they too would love to see me.

His home was about twenty-eight miles away and I knew I would not dare to ask for half a day off, even though I had now been at my job over six months. My off-duty was three evenings every two weeks. One Sunday evening, two Wednesday evenings. This I explained, so if he wished to see me he would have to visit me on my evening off.

He did.

How shy we were on our first meeting in four years! He was thin as I had always known him, about two inches taller than I. I was only five foot two inches. It seemed he had not grown in the years between and now he had an artificial leg. He walked well with only a slight limp, I noticed as we went down the road, but he had a walking stick.

He explained that he had had the leg only a matter of weeks. Before that he had been on crutches. He had these at home and sometimes he used them at weekends. His leg was very tender where the skin had been sewn up, he said.

In answer to my questions, "Are you fixed up with a job? Surely you're not ready to go to work yet?" He said, "No, I'm not fixed up but the pit owners are bound to give me a job if I want one. I have applied and have been told, in view of my wounds," and he pulled a wry face, "they will see what can be done."

We found a restaurant and went in and ordered a pot of tea and some toast, I remember. But I had only one cup of tea — I had eaten at my job. Could I call it home? It was the only home I had, seeing I could not go to my father's home and I did not want my sister's. I suppose, where my work was, that was my home.

We spent two hours together and, as the last train left at about nine o'clock, we walked to the station and sat in the waiting room and talked.

I did not want him to walk too much on my account and perhaps make his leg painful. He said he had wanted to see me for such a long time. He used to wonder if we would ever meet again, seeing that he never heard from me all that long time. He wondered had I got a boyfriend? I said I hadn't.

"Have you had any boyfriends apart from me?"

"Go along, David. I've had one boyfriend for a short while: only he wasn't a real boyfriend." I laughed. "We never even kissed."

"Have I got to believe that?" David said.

"You must please yourself," I said. "I have been here just over six months. Before that I was keeping house for my father and you know him, don't you? He allowed no followers!"

We both laughed.

The train came and he went aboard. I watched it go out and then turned for home.

He had said he would write soon.

So life went on. Me doing my job looking after the children, taking them out, playing with them on the nursery floor, telling them stories, washing, ironing; having a chat with Jessie in the evenings when she was on duty as well as I and enjoying my new interest in life — David.

He wrote about twice a week and managed to come to see me on my evening off-duty. This went on for another four months. I had never been able to go to see his parents. I could not ask for a day off or even half a day. You did not do these things — Mrs Walters's eyebrows would have shot up.

One evening, when David came to see me, he said he had a surprise. He had got a job at the coal mine.

"Not underground, David? You couldn't do it."

"No, not underground. Your cousin, Seth Williams, is under-manager, he has been helpful."

David told me that a big turbine engine had been installed at a cost of £34,000, in a very large building specially built to house it. This engine would be used to pump air down into the mine. It would be used constantly, every hour round the clock, and there would be four men on duty doing an eight-hour shift for three shifts a day. This machine would cut out ten smaller machines and would take much less men. He was to be one of the men to help drive it. He would be starting work the next week.

He came on the following Sunday and told me all about the 'wonder engine'. He liked the work and it wasn't hard.

He loved me, he had told me so in his letters, and he wanted to marry me. His mother and dad would welcome me. We could live with his people as Thomas had left home and married a widow.

I said I would have to think about it all. If I married him I would have to have my parents' consent, seeing I was only twenty. My father had not approved of me 'talking to that boy' when I was thirteen. He used to make me go indoors when he saw me talking to David. I could not see him giving permission for me to marry David, or anyone else for that matter!

The days were now getting longer and warmer. When David came we would go into the gardens close by and sit very

143

closely on the seat near the lake. We would talk and kiss when no one was looking. In the evenings, when it was dusk, down near the station where there were no lights, we stood in a close embrace. We loved each other dearly.

22

A week later I had a letter from home, written by my father. This was the first letter I had had from him since I had left him so suddenly. Mother wrote to me; perhaps he didn't always know when she did write. His letter was a great surprise.

He said my sister Rachel had written to them. She had felt it her duty to tell them that I had resumed my friendship with David Broome. She thought we were serious and suspected that we would want to get married. David Broome had been badly wounded and she thought if I considered marriage I would be making a great mistake. Was this true?

I do not think I was ever more furious with anyone than I was with my sister at that moment. I knew that I would have had to write home to acquaint my parents with what I was doing and tell them about David. I hadn't yet done so because I had not thought it necessary but if I decided to marry David I had intended to write.

To be fair, even if David had not been wounded in the war, I could not have seen my father giving his consent. He would not consent to me marrying anyone. So, I would have to wait another eight months until I was twenty-one.

I made up my mind to see my sister as soon as possible to tell her what I thought of her.

In the meantime I realised I would have to give David a lot of serious thought before I finally made up my mind to marry him. I knew he had this job on the turbine engine. He had said it was not a hard job; could he keep it up? Women did not go out to work — a miner's wife had to stay at home. If they had a family she had to care for the children; if they had none, the miner married a woman to keep her, to be in his home and look after him. The miner is a proud man. Anyway, as mining was the sole work in the area, apart from shop assistants, there was no work even if a woman wished it so far as I could see. So, if David fell ill I would not be able to help out with expenses. True, he had twenty-five shillings a week, it was something, but not enough to keep us. So what? Yes, we would marry. I loved him.

Before seeing David again, I visited my sister. I will not bother to describe the row we had. Lots of nasty things were said and I walked out — not to return to her house for a very long time.

I did not ask for my father's consent. I knew I would not get it.

When I told David we would have to wait until I was twenty-one, he agreed. We decided that the day after I was twenty-one we would be married.

So time went by. The little Walters boys seemed to grow quickly. Ivor was now going to school, his daddy taking him each morning, his mummy leaving work to bring him home. Now we had a new baby, a little sister for the boys, little Sarah. She was a pretty little thing with fair hair, and now two months old.

Mrs Walters no longer went to the Bridgend shop. She stayed at home except when she went occasionally to her husband's studio in town.

She bathed the baby in the mornings while I got Ivor ready for school and gave both boys breakfast, then the baby was left in my care. Little Joseph no longer used the perambulator; it belonged now to baby Sarah, and he walked out with me.

One Saturday I took the two boys and the baby out walking. It seemed that Ivor had picked up some bad habits since starting school. He was very aggressive towards Joseph, often hitting him. He was rude to me too and disobedient. This morning, he was very naughty and kept running away from me with the pram and little Joseph and going out on to the road into the traffic. It was not easy to get him off the road as I had the baby and perambulator. Now, little Joseph followed him out on to the road after Ivor had come back to me and gone out again. I had to put the pram against a shop window and grab the two boys and bring them back to safety. I threatened to tell their mother and I did so, feeling she would scold them and stop them doing what they had, in case of accident.

But instead, she ordered both boys down into the coal cellar which was completely dark. I was shocked. They were terrified.

Mrs Walters told Jessie to bring her dinner into the dining room and before she went into the room said, "Get your dinner from the kitchen and take it into the nursery, nurse."

I didn't. I went down to the children. As soon as I got down to them they clung to me and stopped crying.

Mrs Walters realised there was no crying from the cellar. She went to the nursery and found I was not there. She came to the top of the cellar steps and called down, "Are you down there, nurse?"

"Yes, madam, I am."

"How dare you! All of you come up at once."

We went up the steps and I sent the children into the nursery. Then I turned to Mrs Walters.

"How dare you go down the cellar when I am trying to punish the children after you complained!"

"Madam, how dare you send those children to be terrified in the dark. You could have told them not to go out into the traffic again. You could have stopped their sweets for a day or two. But to put them down there in the dark! I'll never complain to you again. This is the first time I have ever complained, the first time the children have behaved as they did this morning. I am sure they won't do it again." So saying I turned and went into the nursery.

The children's faces were dirty from tears and rubbing their grubby fists in their eyes. Both had slipped on the coal.

I took them up and washed them, then took them to the nursery. I collected their dinners and my own from the kitchen and soon we were busy eating and, I hoped, all in a better frame of mind.

Later we went out walking. They never wandered from me again.

My mother and I continued to write to each other. She said Father was busy now in the garden and soon it would be time for hay-making. The trees were well-laden with apples and pears. The walnut tree looked as though it would be producing some nuts.

Every Sunday morning men my father knew called. They would all go into the barn and settle down on the loose hay round the barrels. They would just sit there and get drunk. Your father too, she said; she had got so mad the other Sunday. She had cooked the Sunday dinner all ready for one o'clock, but no one in the barn made a move to go. So, at one-thirty she went out there and asked them didn't they have a home to go to?

She said, "I said to your father, 'Robert, if you are not inside for your dinner in five minutes I will put it all away and you will get no dinner.'"

I was very amused at Mother's letter. I did not feel from my mother's letters that my father was feeling too badly towards me now.

On pressure from David I decided to ask Mrs Walters for an afternoon off as well as my evening off. I wanted to go and see David's parents. I had been fourteen when I saw them last. Mrs Walters was not too willing to allow the afternoon and evening off-duty but I got it.

It was a happy reunion and David's parents were as kind in their welcome as they had been to me when I was so much younger. David's mum had made various kinds of cakes and we dawdled over tea, talking about their other three sons and two daughters and their children. I talked about myself, the children I was nurse to and my parents, and time passed and it was soon time to make my departure.

David's mother had not aged much. She was the same genial person, who, being North Walian, still mixed her English with Welsh words when she spoke. She never seemed to be able to express herself without a mixture of the two languages.

David's father was English. He had been badly hurt whilst working in the mine. A fall of coal had practically buried him. When they managed to extricate him he was in a very bad state and was rushed to hospital straight from the mine. He was found to have severe stomach damage and was never able to go to work in the mine again. He had received some compensation and David's mother had opened a small shop in her front parlour but David's dad, having nothing to do now, raided the till too often for cash to go to the pub and so the shop was closed.

I remember feeling very sorry for Mrs Broome. I believed her when she told me how hard she had worked to keep that little shop going: making cakes of various kinds, even pickling onions in big jars. People would come, or send their children, for a few pence-worth of onions or pickled cabbage, which she also did. She made a brew which she called 'small beer'. For this she would go out with a basket to where the stinging nettles grew. She would snip the tops off the nettles, wash them, then put them in a large boiler over the fire. After the boiling was done she would strain the liquid off. She owned a large earthenware pan and into this went the liquid, yeast and other concoctions. After it had fermented, this was strained and bottled. She did this not only for the shop she had had before I knew her, but she did it and sold the beer for years after I had married David.

My father wrote to me to say that he hoped I would think very carefully about marrying David. To consider his disability. Having been gassed and shrapnel-wounded it did not sound as if David had much hope of being able to work and keep me and any possible children we might have. He urged me again to think carefully.

I had written a further letter home, saying I intended to marry and was prepared to wait. But, about two months before I was twenty-one, I suppose under my mother's influence, my father wrote to say that, as I was determined to marry David, I could go ahead and fix things.

I was very busy. I had been saving what I could from my wages for some time, and had bought several things for my 'bottom drawer'. Also I decided that I would get a dress for my wedding; a soft mauve dress with a closs-fitting bodice. The skirt of the dress was in three frills, each frill a little deeper than the other. Dress and shoes to match took two months' wages — every penny of it. My mother, on the quiet, sent me five pounds; no doubt money that she had earned and saved when she was working in Coventry. This I kept until I was married, and spent on some of the household goods that were needed. I was sure David was saving too, and would be able to provide much of the other necessary goods.

So my notice was given to Mrs Walters. I was sorry to leave the children. I was fond of them.

Mrs Walters gave me sheets and pillow-cases for which I was grateful and surprised at her generosity. Jessie gave me a tea-pot and stand.

I arrived at David's home two days before the wedding. There was much to do: cakes, sausage rolls, jellies, blanc-manges of all colours to be made. A large cake was waiting to be marzipanned and iced.

It was decided that we would share the house of my to-be-parents-in-law and I was quite happy about this. We were to have two rooms, bedroom and sitting room, with full use of the kitchen. Bathrooms there were not. The bath was, in every working-class house, a big wooden tub. You just filled the copper with water, got the tub into the kitchen, locked the intervening doors to keep out intruders, and enjoyed your bath!

On the morning of the wedding David and I received twenty-five pounds gratuity money from the Government. Somehow, it all got spent, to make the wedding feast a bit more sumptuous. David's mum seemed to bring, besides the big family of relations I had married into, all the people in the street. By the next day there was only one pound note, one ten shilling note and a few coppers left in David's pocket.

Still, it was a lovely wedding day, although my parents did not come — they could not leave Woodlands because the livestock had to be attended to.

23

I was now settled and happy with David and his parents. I asked my mother-in-law to teach me to cook some of the fancy things she excelled in. I helped her with the house-work. Sometimes when David and I went to the market she would come to have a look round and buy things for our own house. She would buy material from the stalls to make dresses for the children of the family. The family would buy these dresses and she would buy more material. After she had shown the neighbours the dresses she began to get orders from them, and so I became involved in helping with the sewing. I also helped with the pickling: preparing onions and cutting up red cabbage, and soon I was doing more work for my mother-in-law than I had time to do my own and have leisure. When David came home, though, my time was devoted to him and I kept to my own comfortable little sitting room.

He was working well. He liked his job but, often, as soon as he came home he was glad to take his artificial leg off, bathe, change his clothes, settle down to a meal and rest in the evening minus his leg. He liked me to read to him. He said he understood better to be read to, rather than read himself.

The months passed by. With David working, his wages were quite good, and we also had his pension of twenty-five shillings a week. We were happy and enjoyed life.

Arrangements to pay the rent of the house had been made by David with his parents. As he worked at the mine, coal was cheap: we could have fifteen hundredweight of coal every six weeks for about ten shillings. So that kept Mother-in-law warm as well as us.

David used to talk bitterly about the loss of his leg. He had been used to swimming, cycling, boxing, climbing and now he could do none of these things. It worried him a lot.

We decided to buy a cycle to see how well he could get along. I persuaded him to borrow Thomas's first, and if he got along with it then to buy one for himself. He found he could manage so got one of his own.

Very soon at weekends he would spend hours cycling and would come home boasting how many miles he had ridden. He would remove his artificial leg and, although he wore a stump sock, his leg would be bleeding where the skin had been sewn over the stump. It took me some time to convince him that if he tortured his leg with such treatment and had to stay at home to recover he would find he could not keep his job. He would listen, and would try to settle down, but often he was restless and every now and then he would go for longer rides than he should, with dire consequences. Although he seldom took a day off work, he would become irritable with himself and was not always easy to cope with.

My father-in-law would involve David in card games — Gin Rummy, Whist and such like. As this mostly needed four people I was taught to play too and David would go down to his brother Thomas and persuade him to play, or else George, another brother who lived close by. Many evenings were spent this way, and at least David was resting. I, for one, was pleased to be raked in to play, if it kept him happy.

I forgot to mention that, at the time of our marriage, I found that the Broome family were keen Spiritualists. The two older brothers, David's two sisters along with Mother — and Father-in-law attended the Spiritualist meetings which were held twice weekly in a large room over a public house. It was not surprising, therefore, that David and I were raked in to go along with the family.

Although David and his father attended these meetings, they used to say it was all a lot of tripe, when they were by themselves.

I, myself, was deeply interested, and in the 'circles' that followed the usual church services and hymn singing when clairvoyance was given. One night I was quite shaken by a medium whom I had never seen before. The lights as always were dimmed. We sat in a circle and the medium walked slowly round close to the 'sitters' and, when she came to me, she said, "I wish you to take your mind right away, to a place many miles from here. A place where you have lived. I gather you lived in the country, in a farming area."

"Yes."

She went on to describe my uncle's farm, a black and white old house with thatched roof: the dog, horse, the cattle and chickens, she described it all as well as I could have done. She described the kitchen and some of the furniture, all of which I had seen on my visits to my aunt and uncle.

Then she described my aunt.

"Do you know the lady I refer to? Was she a relation?"

"Yes."

"She passed away quite soon after you got to know her."

The things she told me could only be known by me and I could not but believe that there really was and is something in Spiritualism. Since then I have attended many meetings over the years. I am a medium myself, not of any great standing, but I remain a confirmed Spiritualist.

The exasperations and frustrations that David endured, because he felt unable to do the things he had so much enjoyed doing in the past, made him feel so often, as he said, 'just half a man', made life not always too happy. The black moods he fell into worried me and annoyed his father. Sharing a house with us, my father- and mother-in-law knew of the little outbursts that happened occasionally. But, between these upsets, life was good and we were very happy. When David overcame these moods he would be very· contrite, apologising most abjectly. But, though these moods passed, they were always near the surface ready to spring up at any moment.

We went walking one day through the woods that came down the back of the row of houses where we lived. It was bluebell time. The woods were carpeted in great patches with them. David decided he must pick a lot of them and when I said I would help he said, "No. I'll pick them and you must sit down on the grass and I will bring them to you to hold on your lap."

So I sat down as he bid me and, when he had picked quite a bunch, I said that surely he had picked enough. But he said he wanted some for his mother, and his two sisters as well. On another occasion when we went walking in the woods we came down to the river Taff. Suddenly he decided he must have a swim. I protested that he had no swimming trunks. He said he would go into the river without. Having found a secluded spot, he hastily stripped, and, leaving his artificial leg with me, he hopped down into the river from the shallow side. He crawled out further and was soon in deep water.

I was very frightened because, had anything gone wrong, there was no one in sight. I had never seen David swimming: I had only heard him talking about his fondness for it. But now, there he was out in deep water, swimming, with only one leg and the stump of the other. I need not have worried. He was quite expert. His lost leg made no difference.

He floated on his back and stuck his stump up straight, then he would roll over, and swim normally. He turned somersaults and his seat would stick up for an instant out of the water as he turned over. Then he suddenly dived underwater and emerged about fifteen to twenty yards up-river.

It was useless to call to him to come out of the water, but I waved my arms to draw his attention. I knew he would leave the cool water only when he was ready.

When he had had enough for one day he started to make for the bank; swimming as near the water's edge as he could; crawling over the stones where the water was shallow and, finally, standing on his one foot and hopping to where I was sitting. "I can swim! I can swim! I can swim as good as ever I did!" he shouted as he came towards me. He was cold and wet; he never had much colour but now his face was drained and white.

I thought, how can he dry himself? We had a couple of handkerchiefs between us. I suddenly thought of my waist-length petticoat. I looked around, could see no one in sight, pulled up my dress, pushed the petticoat down, took it off and passed it to David. He wiped himself as best he could.

He dressed himself, after fixing his leg to the harness he had to wear round his waist with straps up over his shoulders. We started for home after I had rolled up the now very wet petticoat and the two handkerchiefs, into as small a bundle as I could.

I said to David, "I hope no one comes down the road towards us, the sun is behind us and anyone walking towards us will be able to see through my dress and see my bloomers underneath!"

We both giggled as we walked. We passed only a lady and gentleman; how much they saw through my thin dress I do not know — nor did I care very much. Soon we were home, and David went straight into his mother's big kitchen to tell her about his swimming. I said he had stayed in the water far too long for a first time and that he was shivering when he got up to the bank beside me.

Mother-in-law scolded him. "You could have caught your death, silly boy you are. Don't you know you are not what you used to be? Not that you ever were strong." So she went on.

I thought, the worst thing you could have said was: 'Don't you know you are not what you used to be?' David was trying so hard to tell himself, to prove to himself, that he *was* what he used to be. That he could do what he used to do was what he wanted to believe.

At that moment, Father-in-law came down the garden path and into the house. David told him that he had been in the river and how easy it was to swim.

Father-in-law said what I had hoped he would say, "Well done, boy. How did it go?"

"Oh, fine, Dad, fine. I can swim as good as I ever did."

After a few moments we went into our own quarters and soon we were both drinking hot tea. I hoped it would help to warm up his body but next day he was ill and unable to go to work.

It was quite two weeks before he was fit again and he refused to see a doctor. He did, though, decide not to go into the river again until summer advanced and the water was warmer.

One morning after David and I had been married for fifteen months, my mother-in-law asked me how I was, and I said I felt not too grand at all. I had been sick and had put it down to the fact that I had eaten something that had upset me.

A day or two later I had gathered up the washing, and carried the things into the scullery. The copper was full of boiling water and I was about to start putting the clothes into the big wooden tub. I bent down to soap the soiled clothes and suddenly felt giddy. I staggered into my mother-in-law's room.

"Oh, Mother, I feel awful," I gasped.

She looked keenly at me. "I know what you need — a little water and vinegar, or a pickled onion. Have you got any in your cupboard?" She marched off into my living room and came back with the pickle jar. She poured a tablespoonful of vinegar into a cup and about the same of water.

I sat and sipped the raw-tasting potion and — strange to say — I wasn't sick but soon felt well enough to finish the washing and hang it on the line. After which I emptied the remaining water out of the copper, cleared the fire grate, emptied and dried the big tub, then went into the living room and sat down.

"Having a cup of tea, are we?" my mother-in-law said as she came in. "Mind if I have one too?"

She sat down in the armchair opposite me, and after a minute or two said, "You know, I think you're going to have a baby."

Of course she was right, and my baby daughter whom I named Amy Margret was born the following March. She was a small baby, perfect in body, with a lot of dark brown hair. We were all delighted with her, and when she started to walk, her grandfather spent a lot of time with her out in the garden, watching her play. She talked very plainly, and one day something had happened to make the old fellow do a swear. Amy stared at him. "Grandad naughty," she said.

24

The big coal strike of the early Twenties came. The coal-mine owners said there had to be a drop in wages.

Although wages had risen during the war, living costs had increased too and remained high when the war ended: the cost of food, clothes and everything one bought. Now, with the mine owners saying wages would have to come down, the miners all over the country came out on strike and I think, at that time, everyone was in sympathy with them.

I do not know how some people managed. There was no unemployment pay. Men would go to the coal tips and scrape around for coal for their own use. The mines were completely on stop. The horses which were used underground to pull the 'journeys' of coal up to the cages which took the coal to the surface had all been brought up and taken out to graze on green fields. Some of these horses had never seen daylight and all of them had to wear blinkers for a few days until they grew accustomed to it.

Soup kitchens were opened. People could go there with large jugs and get soup to take home to their family.

Then there was trouble amongst the miners. They rioted. People in the Rhondda valley really went to town, smashing windows of municipal buildings and caused so much disturbance that (I believe) the Government set up a fund. People were able to collect a few shillings per head and so were able to keep body and soul together. The times were really bad.

Rents mounted up. No one could pay the modest rent of about eight shillings per week for a three-bedroomed house and, over the six months the pits were idle, debts rose.

The mine owners stuck to their guns. They, at least, were not going short, they could still afford to wait. The miners had been offered a wage that was a drop of ten shillings for each working day; so the miners stayed out on strike for six months.

Someone had a wonderful idea. The miners needed something to interest them, something to take their minds off the desperate times everyone was going through, to keep them away from the riots and violence which erupted as the men grew more desperate. So the idea was born. Why didn't the miners take up interests, such as organising Fancy Dress parades?

In the mining districts parties of men gathered together, one group dressed up as comic footballers; one used to carry what was a baby, and, as the men walked down the streets, they would stop and the man with the so-called baby would sit down in the road to change the baby's nappy. Another party became the 'Wild Men from Borneo'. They marched entirely naked except for loincloths, their bodies coloured a chocolate brown. They wore strings of coloured beads round their necks and ankles. They even walked barefoot to make the whole thing look more natural, and they carried a canoe.

Each party would be made up of eighteen or twenty men and the wonderful ideas these Welsh men invented for their processions needed seeing to be believed. Collections were taken as the processions marched down the streets. Pennies were given by those who could find a coin and the cash collected went to buy food for the soup kitchen to enable folks to collect the daily ration of soup, even on Sunday. How kind and how dedicated were the voluntary helpers who worked so hard in these soup kitchens for seven days a week. So typical of the Welsh people amongst whom I was born, and lived, and respected and loved.

David and I were lucky, at least we had the twenty-five shillings a week which kept us in food, cheap and simple though it was.

We all survived: the strike ended; the men were beaten. They went back to work on the mine owners' terms and, whilst I cannot speak about the wages of other men, David's pay actually was dropped from sixteen shillings per day to eight shillings. Some had an even bigger drop in wages.

There was a Miners' Federation set up to fight for the miners' rights, but I believe people working in the mines were not forced to join, so the Federation was not strong enough to fight the mine owners, when the strike happened. After the strike the miners realised they had made a mistake in not belonging to the Federation and, the strike being over, they joined up and soon became a force to be reckoned with and, although not called the Miners' Federation now, it is a very powerful backing for miners' rights, for good or ill.

When David and I married, as I have said, we undertook to pay the rent for the house and to supply coal for us all. Mother-in-law received some help from the family and, with what she earned with her sewing and dressmaking for neighbours, she did not do too badly.

The house was, of course, in Father-in-law's name but, a week after we were married we found that we had to pay an arrears in rent which amounted to about six pounds. As the rent of the house was only eight shillings per week Mother-in-law must have let the rent man be turned away many times to mount up such a debt.

There were hot words between David and his mother and I was very embarrassed. I said, "Well, all right, we will pay the arrears too." As my mother-in-law saw the rent man as usual and paid thē rent we gave her each week, we also paid off some of the arrears each time until it was cleared up.

I, too, kept an account of what we paid off in arrears and in weekly rent and so it was a bit of a shock when, about three months later, I came upon the rent book and discovered we still owed over six pounds. Mother seemed to have missed paying the rent regularly.

I told David about this and he demanded to see the rent book and found what I had said was correct. There were sharp words again. I was upset at being the cause of the quarrel but I knew I had been right to speak to David. It seemed to me that we were always going to be owing rent, the way David's mother was going on, and I felt, instead of battening on to David with his poor health, she should have

159

paid over the rent and arrears each week as it was given to her.

The result of this quarrel between mother and son was that David insisted on seeing the rent book each week, to make sure that what he had given had really been paid.

So the arrears came down, according to how much we could give his mother over and above the rent each week. Some weeks we were able to pay more than others.

My little Welsh mother-in-law had one weakness — she loved clothes and was always well-dressed. Although she did dressmaking she did not make her own clothes; she preferred to *buy* her own clothes.

On several occasions when we had gone to do the weekend shopping, Mother had blown nearly all she had in her purse on a dress, skirt or, on one occasion, a costume that cost twenty-five shillings. This left her with little money to buy the Sunday joint, which cost about half-a-crown.

This, I could not understand. My ma-in-law had always to me seemed so level-headed and sensible. I was quite shaken. At my own home, Mother had always kept a good table and we lived as well at the end of the week as we did at the beginning. We had, when we were all living at home, three men working in the coal mine, my father and two older brothers, and they had to be well-fed, to do such hard work and so the rest of us were well-fed too.

I was glad David was not interested in spending a whole evening in the pub like his brother Thomas. He preferred to spend Saturday evening at the cinema or, if it was too wet a night, we would talk together. Sometimes I would read to him. He often fancied a book from a bookstall and, having bought it, I knew that was the next in line to be read.

But, often, he talked about the war, about his experiences; and, as I listened, I thought what awful things to see and go through which ended for him when his leg was blown off when he was only eighteen years and six months old. Now, I thought, he goes through another kind of hell, when he is often forced to stay away from work because his leg bleeds. These were days when he would get out the pair of crutches from under the stairs. Often he would use them for the whole of Sunday so that he could go to work the following week.

One night, he told me, they had been ordered to go forward. (The Germans were supposed to be about a mile away behind a range of hills.) They had first to cut a whole lot of barbed wire which was about two hundred yards away. Some volunteers went to cut the wire but they were shot immediately by German snipers. They decided to wait until dusk when another party of six went out to cut the wire. With them was a Captain Cupit. The snipers attacked again and some of the men were shot, including Captain Cupit. Two men managed to crawl back but the Captain lay dead, sprawled over the barbed wire. Volunteers were called for later when it was thought, perhaps, they could take a chance on recovering the body but these men either died or were badly injured. Eventually, the Captain's body *was* recovered and David was one of the party who brought the body back to their lines.

One night, when the house was all quiet, we had been in bed for about three hours or more when suddenly I felt a pressure on my chest. I awoke to find David, who had been sleeping on the inside of the bed close to the wall, climbing over me. He hopped to the bedroom door and opened it. Then, as if he were looking at something, he gave a most terrifying yell. "My God, my God, they are coming!" He shouted these words twice. I got out of bed and went to him; I had been fully awake the moment I felt the pressure on my chest. I put my arm around him and said, "They are gone now, love, come back to bed."

"They're there. They're coming back," said David.

"No, love, they're gone."

He turned slowly and went back to bed and I climbed in beside him covering myself and him with the bedclothes.

Next morning I said to him, "No more talking about the war, especially at bedtime. You scared the living daylights out of me last night."

"Why? What happened last night?"

I told him and he stared at me, not believing me. At last he said, "Don't tell lies. I did nothing of the sort."

"All right, you can ask your dad, he must have heard you. You had a nightmare," I said quietly.

We never said any more about it, but I have a feeling he did speak to his father when they were alone.

It is so many years now since my dear little Welsh mother- and father-in-law departed this life; but I love them still and their memory will live with me until I die.

I can see my mother-in-law now, as she used to be in the days we lived together.

Every morning after breakfast, she would clear away the dishes, tidy up her own rooms and then secure her little black hat with two long hatpins. Then she would put on her 'turnover' — a black shawl with deep fringes. This she would fasten close to her neck with an old-fashioned brooch, which had belonged to her mother, and away she would go around to her daughter's house; either to Maria's or Polly's, or to both, for a cup of tea and a chat; no doubt to take any news if anything was worth talking about and to bring news back home.

My father-in-law, because he wasn't earning, got little in the way of pocket money, so he was always glad of little 'perks' now and then.

"Dad," I would say, "Are you going down town this morning?"

"No, my gell, I wasn't. Is there something you wanted?"

"Well, yes, I wanted one or two things from the 'Maypole' and I don't want to go down today, I want to help Mother with the sewing." Or it would be "to help Mother peel the onions for her pickling."

"Oh, well, I'll go, my gell. I'll be ready in about ten minutes. Get the list ready."

He would be ready and I would give him the list and money for the goods. According to how much cash I had, I would give him fourpence halfpenny to buy an ounce of Franklin Tobacco or if it was a Friday morning and payday was

Saturday, I might not be too flush for cash myself and might only be able to give him twopence halfpenny for half an ounce of tobacco.

He would say, sometimes, "Don't tell your mother, will you, or she'll cut me short on my pocket money on Saturday." And, of course, I did not tell. That was our secret.

One day Mother said, "I don't know why, but if *you* ask your father-in-law to go down town for you, he goes like a shot; but if *I* ask him he's never willing to go."

We all walked down to the market one day (four miles), Mother, Dad, David and I. There were no buses or tramcars. True, we could have walked to the station and gone by train but, as Dad would say, "While we walk to the station we could be halfway there." So we would walk, all four of us.

This day when we went there were some geese for sale and some baby goslings too. David fell in love with the little yellow creatures and wanted to buy some. His father said, and I agreed, that the goslings would cost a lot to feed. Father said, "Geese needs a field then they can graze their own living. They eat lots of grass and we've only got the back garden. You will have to buy all their food and they are big eaters. They won't pay you, don't buy them, boy."

But David had to buy them and we came home with six little goslings in a wooden box. As it was a Saturday when we bought them we had to feed them on bread and milk until Monday when the shops would be open.

David and Father-in-law went round the family and managed to get some wood from one and the other. They knocked up a little house at the top of the garden and the goslings lived there and grew.

David loved them and Father-in-law used to go up the garden with his pipe puffing away and sit on an old box to watch the geese. David bought some more wood and with his dad's help enlarged the goslings' hut.

The goslings grew to full size and were lovely with their long white neck and breast and slate-coloured wings.

David had tarred the house which the geese lived in. The silly things went rubbing up around the sides of it before it was dry and they got tar all down the front of their white breasts. David was very upset until he thought of a solution. "Go up and ask Alfred for some petrol," he said to me. "A drop in a tin will do. Tell him what you want it for."

I brought back about a pint I would guess. David held each goose between his knees and, while I caught hold of its neck, he rubbed its feathers with a piece of old rag soaked in the petrol until he got most of the tar off. When that job was finished as we looked at them waddling back to their house, we saw they were staggering drunkenly. It must have been the fumes from the petrol.

As Father had prophesied they had cost a lot to keep but we intended to have one for Christmas and the others we sold. David's brother, George, said he would have a raffle of two of them at the public house and it would fetch us a good price. What price they fetched we never knew because we did not ever receive the cash.

We still went to the Spiritualist meetings every week and sometimes we had a 'circle' in the house. Bessie, my sister-in-law, was the medium. She was very clever and used to go into a deep trance. She told me once, "You will receive a letter from an elderly lady (she described my mother) and she will tell you of the death of an old man. The old man lives quite near to her."

"Not a relative?" I asked.

"No, there is no family connection. Because of him you will have news of a lady who lived with him, but does not live with him now; has not lived with him for a long time."

I wondered about this for some days. Before the week was out my mother wrote me a letter.

She told me that old Mr Pressley had been found dead in bed and that she had been meaning to tell me for some time that Ada who had left him about eighteen months before, was now in the workhouse in Badminton. She had been found wandering, cold and hungry, after she had left old Mr Pressley, with nothing but what she stood up in, and had been taken into the workhouse. She had asked the police to keep her whereabouts from the old man and they had respected her wish.

I thought about it all after reading my mother's letter and I came to the conclusion that although workhouses in 1921 were very dreary places I felt she was better off than she had ever been. I hoped so.

25

I think we had been living with Mother-in-law for about two years when our second daughter was born. Emily Lillian was a bonny little girl, getting into everything, and between the two little girls there was never a dull moment. Amy loved her small sister, and loved to rock the wooden cradle that had once been hers and was now her sister's. Only she would rock the cradle a little too vigorously and I had to tell her, "You must go gently, like this" and show her how gentle, "or you will have the baby tipped on to the floor." Their grandfather was always willing to sit in the garden and watch both children when Emily was big enough to play with the few toys they had or nurse the big rag doll their grandma had made for them.

David had become restless. He was often away from work, not always because of his leg which still troubled him, but it seemed as if he wanted to get away from his family. So, one day, when I was writing to my parents I told them how we felt and said that if they ever heard of a little cottage with a fair-sized garden in Dilwyn, perhaps we would be able to get it. As they lived on the spot they might be able to put in a word for us perhaps.

David was very much in favour of this move and, about six months later, when tenancies changed, mother wrote to say that a nice old black and white cottage in good condition, had become available. It had a well at the front and gardens front and back. The rent was two shillings and sixpence per week but paid monthly. The farmer did not want a workman, the cottage had no strings. The farmer had six sons and they were all living at home and all working on the farm so it was for rent only.

And so David gave up his job at the pit and we moved back to Dilwyn. On the day of departure I wanted to check to see that we had everything, but was forbidden to do so by David. I was to look after the children while David and his brother loaded the van. When we at last arrived at our lovely cottage in Dilwyn, it was to discover that the beautiful oval table and a hanging lamp had been left behind.

I found too, when we arrived, that pots and pans would have to be hung on a sway over the fire. My saucepans were unsafe to put straight on to a coal fire and there would be little chance of finding wood, so I would have to buy some pots with handles. There was of course no electricity or gas, so we used paraffin lamps and candles.

We had three bedrooms, three rooms downstairs and a long room the length of the house where we could keep the coal at the bottom end. It seemed that was where the outgoing tenants had kept their coal. The top end, David said, could be for him to put his tools; he seemed to have quite a lot although until now he had not used them much (except to make the goose house).

Upstairs, too, there was a long room and in this room was a trap door secured by a large bolt in the ceiling of the room below. We wondered what that room had been used for and, on enquiring from the neighbour some weeks later, were told that years before people who had lived there had used the upper long room for storing cider in barrels. After studying the size of the trap door we both agreed that barrels (not so big as father's fifty-gallon barrels) could be hauled up through the trap door. The walls were thick and strong, the floor boards solid and firm, fixed on beams each about four to six inches thick.

When we could afford to buy paint, the walls of the living rooms downstairs we painted white, and the beams black. We did one room at a time.

The bedroom floors had never had a carpet, indeed, all the people I knew and the houses of the miners never had carpets. The kitchen-cum-living room in David's mother's house and all the houses in the street were stone-flagged and thus had to be scoured and scrubbed. In front of the fire we had a big, coarse mat which was rolled up and shaken then put back into place.

This house we had taken over was the same: stone-flagged in the first two rooms downstairs; the third room and the 'long room' as we always called it, were bricked, some of which were broken and not easy to walk on.

The rooms upstairs had bare wooden floors — for us as well — except for the two mats I had made at David's house and brought to our new home with us. These went each side of our double bed and except for a dressing table and a small table by the bed the room was pretty bare. There was an open corner cupboard that had been used for a wardrobe and, after I had cleaned it and painted the wall, we too used it as a wardrobe for us both.

Curtains for two windows I had brought down with me from David's home and, when Mother went into market with Mr Williams who had taken me to the station when I had left my father more than two years before, he also took David and me for a charge of two shillings each and I was able to buy curtains for two more windows. I was pleased in one way that the windows in the bedrooms were not very big — it took less curtaining. I also bought two cooking pots with oval handles. They were made of cast iron, as were the saucepans I had brought with me from David's home.

We only had enough furniture to furnish two rooms — the bedroom and the living room, but the house was now quite comfortable. It was a lovely old house, I thought. The well looked quite like the well in picture book stories of Jack and Jill. The path was cobble-stoned from the house down to the little gate and the small garden in the front had a nice plot of grass in the centre and a border all round with daffodils, primroses and bushes which we were told were Michaelmas daisies.

The back garden we started to dig. We bought seed potatoes. Mother said they should have been in the ground a month before but perhaps if we got going and put them in soon it wouldn't matter much. So we set to on the garden.

Someone had left a garden fork in the coal shed and David started digging while I went to ask Mother if she had a spare one I could borrow, for Woodlands was only ten minutes' walk away.

She said my father would not be needing his fork for that day, but I must take it back in the afternoon in case he wanted to use it.

Father was still working for Mr Dent on odd days. He never went to work for him regularly, only when he came to say he was hard pushed for some special job like hay-making. Then, Father would go for a few days and then he would be home doing his own work.

I borrowed the fork, promising to return it at about three o'clock. Father was not due home until five but, as Mother said, "You never know with him."

So David and I worked hard until the afternoon. When three o'clock came I told David to get on his cycle and return the fork to my mother so she could put it with Father's tools.

That evening David's leg was bleeding again. I suppose the ground was 'stubby' and that aggravated it. So next day I went digging alone.

In two days we had cleared quite a patch of grass and, after digging a ditch, David was able to plant the potatoes in three rows along from end to end.

We worked hard for a week. The weather was fine and warm and we were pleased with ourselves. We dug more; though David had to stop some days because of his leg but, even so, we planted up the whole area with vegetables and marrows. David made a bed and lined it with dead grass and nettles and covered this with light soil before putting in the marrow seed. Later, I was able to make marrow jam. This lasted us a long time and helped out with expenses.

In the autumn there were blackberries in abundance and we both went round the hedgerows, trespassed in some of the farmers' fields, and picked enough berries to make quite a store of jam; I only had to buy the sugar, which cost about threepence a pound. We also picked blackberries for pies and puddings and we did well. But I was unlucky with one lot of berries: I had put them on to boil in my cauldron pot over the open fire, I had added the sugar and was stirring the jam when a large lump of soot fell right into it. It was all spoilt, of course.

Before then, at the end of July, was hop-picking time. Mothers took their children with them into the hop fields and tried to induce them to pick hops, because on the pay that mother and children would earn depended the buying of the children's clothes for the coming winter. But only the older children would work, and that under threat from Mum of what she would do to them if they didn't; even so, more than one of the children at various times got a cuff round the ear — to show she meant what she said.

Although David and I had never been into a hop field, we decided to pack some sandwiches and go to see if we would be allowed to pick hops and earn some cash. We took the children with us and went into the field where we were shown a 'crib'.

This consisted of about five poles which, when erected were tied or fixed up with hessian, the hessian forming a kind of trough. The men picked the 'vines' and brought them to the women standing by the crib. The flowers grew in bunches and each flower had to be picked off separately before being put into the crib. About twice a day, a man came round with a bin in which the picked hops were measured and you received a tin token for each binful you picked. You knew how much each binful was worth to you and, at the end of the hop-picking, you got paid.

The first morning we found tea had been made by the farmer's wife and, if you had a jug or can, you could, when the farmer's wife called 'tea up' go and fill up with hot tea. This happened twice a day. As we had taken no jug or can on this first day we decided when we came on the morrow to rectify this mistake.

We both liked picking the hops. David took a stool he had made with longish legs for easy sitting and I stood by the 'crib'. The hops stained our hands and roughened them, so I decided to look for a pair of gloves I could take with me to save my hands as much as possible.

To me the job was very interesting. It amused me to watch

the parents and children around me and we found the smell of the hops gave us quite an appetite. Of course, we were slow getting the flowers off the vine as we picked them off one by one but, as we watched the experienced pickers, we found they stripped them off by cupping the hand over the bunch. We tried this and found we did much better.

All the people in the hop field lived quite near but in some of the very large hop fields, my mother told me, people came down from London, the farmer having large barns which were put to the visitors' use for sleeping; facilities for cooking, my father had told Mother, were pretty crude. Mr Dent had a large acreage of ground planted with hops so he had to have 'foreigners' in, seeing there would not be enough local people to do the picking.

Hop-growers had to have kilns in which to dry them. This was a specialised job for experienced men, as one could be at a great loss if the drying by fire went wrong and the hops were burned. The kilns gave off a pungent smell which David said was not unpleasant.

My father had also said that the 'foreigners' who came to Mr Dent's farm came every year considered hop-picking as a holiday for the family. The village's one pub did a very good trade whilst they were down for the hop-picking season!

Once you took up the hop-picking you were expected to carry on to the end, there was no leaving off for a day, unless the weather was wet. I believe I am right in saying hops must not be picked in the rain as they become more difficult to dry.

Although I had enjoyed it, and I believe David had too, it had meant working for about seven hours a day. I heard that some of the people had put in longer hours, getting to the field at six o'clock in the morning. David and I usually got there at about nine and left at four in the afternoon. The 'season' which lasted until all the hops had been picked took three weeks, every day except Sunday. At the end of that time we collected our cash and decided to buy some clothes for ourselves and the children; we all needed new footwear.

As the evenings grew longer David became more restless. Outside our window was a very tall fir tree. David said he was sure he had heard an owl up in the tree top and he thought there was a nest up there. I was scornful. I said owls did not nest in trees. I was sure they got into barns!

"No," David said. "They nest in trees and one of these nights I'm going to climb up that tree and see if I can get an owl."

For about three weeks he said no more about it and I thought to myself that he had decided against climbing it. It would have been a dangerous thing to do for a man with two good legs in the daytime. The branches were thick, the tree trunk itself about four feet or more round; but, to climb it at night, in the dark, would be madness. Then, one night when I thought David had gone to the 'cabin in the pines' (the outside lavatory) I thought he was a long time coming back to the house and I went outside and stood in the darkness. I opened the small gate to the garden and looked as best I could down the path, but I could not see him, so I called, "David, where are you?"

From the top of that tree came a voice, "I'm up the tree."

"My God!" I thought.

I tried to keep panic out of my voice. "David, come down, please."

"I'm coming, there's nothing up there so far as I can see."

When he got down, he brushed himself and I could see he'd torn his sleeve.

"David, you do the daftest things. You could have fallen."

"Well, I didn't, so hush and make a cup of tea."

That October, one day at about four in the afternoon, David's father arrived unexpectedly. He had come by train and had walked the six miles from Leominster.

We were both pleased to see the old fellow. He said he had missed us; we had missed him too. David often called into Woodlands to see my mother when he went for his pension, but he never cared to go much when my father was around. I sometimes felt he missed his family, so the old chap was welcome. He had bought a one-way ticket. Mother-in-law was short of cash so she would send his fare home when he told her he was ready to return. It was obvious that Dad had only a few shillings to buy a bit of tobacco and perhaps the odd half pint of beer. He stayed for three weeks and then, having received his fare home by post from Mother-in-law and her request to him to return, he left.

David had made a few attempts to find work on some of the farms, but he found it difficult to work a full week straight off. If he did, then he had to walk on his crutches on the Sunday. It was obvious that the last piece of leg that had been taken off had not been a good job, especially where the skin had been sewn after being pulled round to cover the stump. It was obvious, too, that it would always be troublesome.

To make matters worse, although he had been supplied with two artificial legs so that he would always have one good one if the other needed repair, he was tardy in sending away the leg needing repair, so that often he had *two* legs needing repair. When he did, at last, send one away the other was kept together by will power and pieces of string, until the repaired leg was returned, then it was a work of art to persuade him to send away the second leg. It took about three weeks for repairs and then they were soon needed again. It cost him nothing to post the artificial legs as any postage he had paid was refunded; it was just a matter of getting the thing sent off.

On one occasion when David's leg was away and the other badly in need of repair, my brother Jim paid a visit to Woodlands. On the Sunday morning, he came down to our house and invited David for a drink at the 'Tally-ho' about three miles away. They promised to be back before two o'clock. Jim said he only wanted one pint of beer. I asked how many times he would want his pint glass filled; I knew my brother!

At last, well past two, David and Jim returned and I hurried my brother away to Woodlands — mother never let anyone keep her dinner waiting once she had it ready.

When he had gone, I turned my attention to David. He sat sprawled in the chair, looking very pale and tired.

He felt awful. He had had a couple of pints and then been

sick. But worst of all, his leg had broken down as they were walking home and he had had to take out one of his shoe laces to tie it; then he had to take out the other and managed to get about two miles before both laces broke. "So I had to hold it on. I had to tear open my trouser pocket to put my hand through to hold the leg on."

He took his leg off downstairs along with his trousers and shoes, then hopped upstairs and into bed. When I went up later he was fast asleep.

He came down as it got dusk, and I made tea. I told him I had been upstairs earlier but he was asleep and I thought it better to leave him. I asked him how he felt now.

"Bloody awful. Do you know, I felt like dying, it's no good, booze doesn't suit me. Don't ask me to eat now, love, I'll just have a cup of tea."

I couldn't understand it next morning, he still could not eat and he looked sad.

"I'm fed up. I will have to get my crutches out. How long are they going to take to send my other leg back? How long since we sent it away?"

"Only about ten days and it usually takes three weeks. Can't you do something to your leg that's standing in the corner, just to carry on till it comes back?"

David said he would look at it and when he had drunk his tea I carried it over to him. And there was nothing he could do, so I persuaded him to let me pack it up and take it to the village post office at once so that that repair could be going on before the other leg returned; in that way both legs would be in good order together.

David spent a week using his crutches.

"You know," he said, "I'm sure there are some birds in that nest on top of the chimney."

"I haven't noticed a nest on top of the chimney."

But when I looked again I could really see there was a nest up there.

"David, don't go attempting to climb up to the top of that chimney."

"I didn't say I would, did I?"

"No," I said, "but I know *you*. For God's sake, David, have some sense. Other men with *two* legs don't have to do the silly things you do. What are you trying to do? Because you've lost a leg it doesn't make you less of a man. You don't have to prove yourself; do something useful, that's more sensible."

He sat silent for a long time and I left the room to wash the dishes.

Some days later, one of the artificial legs returned and David was cheerful at the sight of the postman with the parcel. He was soon walking round the house and garden and feeling a new man. The crutches had hampered his movements and he had been very bored.

It must have been about a month later, that he mentioned the nest on the chimney top again.

"That would be empty now, birds grow quickly and they will be gone," I said.

"Yes, I expect so," he said. "One of these days a good wind will blow it down."

I hoped so. But the temptation to climb on to the roof that jutted out over the kitchen was too much and as I was washing up the breakfast dishes one day, I heard a bump out on the grass plot in front of the living room. I rushed out. David had somehow managed to reach the top of the chimney and the empty nest lay on the ground to prove it. He was on his feet and was busily brushing his trousers down. He looked white and shaken but smiled sheepishly.

"You'd better come in and I'll make a pot of tea."

He followed me, sat in his armchair and promptly passed out.

When he came to, slowly, as I gave him some water he said, "All right, love, don't say it."

"Say what?"

"What you want to say," he said.

"Are you all right? That's what I want to say. Where are you hurt?"

He said he had fallen on his back, but he wasn't hurt too much.

175

I wanted to get the doctor in but he would not hear of it and for two or three days, though he protested he was all right, he did not go outside the house and I was sure he had been more hurt than he would say. But, by the weekend, he walked out into the garden and I thought he was walking like he usually did.

Neither of us referred to the fall, or to his climbing the chimney. He had meant to climb up there, I thought, and he had done it so there was nothing to be done about it.

26

At about Christmas time, my mother said she wanted to prepare some dressed fowl to take to the market, to earn some extra spending money, and my father wanted to go into Leominster for the Christmas market too. He had five nice-sized porkers to sell. Mother had been grumbling about having to look after them and the two sows Father kept. She had to feed them when Father was at Mr Dent's.

In the end, it was decided one old sow should go, as well as the porkers.

They asked David and me to go up and stay at Woodlands whilst they were away, as they did not want to leave the place unattended. Having nothing better to do I put the socks I was knitting for David in my bag, and to Woodlands with the children we went.

Father was trying, with Mother's help, and the carrier's to get the pigs up into the lorry, but the pigs had other ideas so we were welcomed as extra help. Father duly departed with the carrier but Mother had a last few words before they left: "Don't you bring any more pigs back, Robert, mind, we will have more in the spring but not now. Our old sow is expecting *hers* in a month or so and that will be enough."

Mother hastily got herself ready and Mr Williams appeared at the gateway. David carried out the big basket in which Mother had packed her chickens, covered with a big white cloth. She climbed into the trap and David stowed the basket under the seat.

"All right, Mum?"

"Yes, all right, now get some dinner for yourselves. There is ham in the larder; help yourselves, and vegetables to fry up, and there's some apple tart. Get yourselves some cider from the barn and mind you turn the tap off properly."

We walked into the house and warmed ourselves by the fire. It was a very cold day. We were to empty the pail of pigswill into the trough for the old sow at about one o'clock and collect the eggs from the two poultry houses, and that was all.

I had told David about the ghostly footsteps I used to hear upstairs (my mother had also heard them) and told him of the money the old man was supposed to have hidden before he went off to the asylum.

David said, "Now we are by ourselves, I want to see if I can find the old man's money."

"For goodness' sake, don't be daft. Don't you think Mother would have found it?"

"Yes, but I may look somewhere where she wouldn't think of."

"Well, how do you propose looking for it? You are not going to interfere with things belonging to my mother, David."

"No, of course not, I want to go round the walls, sound them with a hammer, see if they are hollow that sort of thing . . ."

I was not happy about this, but tapping the wooden walls that closed off the stairs or the wooden walls of the other room would not cause any damage, so I did not worry too much. I was sure David would soon give up and find his efforts fruitless, which he did, and he settled down by the fire with me.

"I wonder where he could have put it?"

"I don't suppose the old man hid any money," I said.

"Well, why does he come back, there must be a reason, otherwise he'd go and settle down and tell himself he's dead!"

"Perhaps his soul doesn't agree he's dead," I said, laughing.

"Perhaps not," said David. Then after some thought, "Wonder where else he could have put it?"

"Out in the orchard or the meadow. Go and dig it all up with a spade, perhaps you will find it. For goodness' sake forget about it, David. This isn't our house. Behave yourself."

So the matter ended, but I still feel that there was money planted by the old man when he had overheard his family discussing putting him into an asylum because he had become mentally deranged. They say an insane person can have periods of light in between the shadows in his mind when his mind becomes clear for a while. I still believe he had buried it somewhere, inside or outside the house and, obviously to me, it was not upstairs, seeing that the heavy footsteps walked through the two bedrooms to the top of the stairs, never to walk down. I felt it was somewhere downstairs, probably even out in the ground and, having buried it, his clouded mind could not remind him.

I feel sure that one day, when that house is taken to pieces and demolished, the secret will be found. That will not be in my lifetime.

At about three o'clock Mother returned with Mr Williams. We heard the horse and trap stop outside the gate and David and I went out to help her bring in her shopping.

"Did you get a good price for your chickens?"

"Yes, I did *very* well. I always go to the same man and he always treats me fairly," said Mother. "I have presents for you both but they are for Christmas so you cannot see them now."

We sat talking and by and by Mother got concerned about Father. At last, we heard the rumble of the cart wheels of the carrier's lorry and we went out to the gate to wait for it.

Father had had a few!

"I've got something in the lorry," said Father. "Help me to unload."

The carrier got down from his vehicle and walked to the tailboard ready to let it down.

"What have you got there, Robert?"

"Come and see."

"We went round to the back and, over the tailboard, a head of a strange sow appeared.

"My God, what has he got now?"

We could all hear the noise of several pigs.

"A sow, and ten pigs, Jane," said my father.

"A sow and ten pigs! He takes in five pigs and a sow and brings me back ten pigs and a sow. It's too much, just too much!" said Mother.

The tailboard was taken down and between us we decanted the pigs on to the yard. After some trouble they were all inside the empty sty.

When the carrier had gone Mother turned on Father. "They look starved, the sow is all bone and skin."

"Yes," said Father. "Poor old thing, but she looks healthy enough. They all went so cheap, I had to buy them. When I looked at them, Jane, and heard how cheap they were, I bid another ten bob for them, and I said to myself, 'Jane will soon get some flesh on the old sow'. You always were a good 'un with animals."

"You'll get nowhere by smarming round me," said Mother.

"Tell you what, Jane. You feed them and put some flesh on the old sow and look after those ten little ones and when they are ready for market, you can have the value of two of the pigs. How's that?"

Mother was silent and I knew Father had won her over.

27

As the days were very short, the mornings cold and frosty and the evenings dark by about four-thirty, David grew more restless. I had run out of books to read to him. He taught me to play cards again, games I did not know and which I did not learn too easily. I suppose it was because I never had any real interest in card playing and the interest faded. We often sat talking about the family. To us both, as far as we were concerned, they might as well be a thousand miles away because we could not afford to visit his people. So one dry, cold Sunday morning, he said, "I think I will ride up home to Abercynon."

"When?"

"Today," said David.

"It's nearly seventy miles and you want to cycle all that way! You know your leg won't stand it. Don't be ridiculous, David. It will be dark early and you know your acetylene lamp is no good, the carbide always seems to get wet too soon, and you will be in the dark on some long, strange road."

The cycle lamp had been an annoyance and a joke too, at times, because it never burned right. I do not know if there were any battery lamps for cycles but we did not possess one.

"Get me some sandwiches done, Bett, and pack me some pyjamas and I'll be on my way. It's ten o'clock now. I could be there round eight o'clock tonight."

"How long will you stay?"

"Don't know. Just about three days, no more. Should be back on Friday or Saturday," said David.

"Oh well, I suppose I shall have to be all right."

David smoked a pipe and I saw he had his tobacco and matches. I had a few shillings which I gave him and I said, "See you are back, David. Your pension is due on Wednesday and I can't draw it. I have no money at all but I know I can borrow from Mother to tide me over. If you are not back on Friday it means, anyway, your pension will have to be held over to the following week. Then you will draw fifty shillings for the two weeks, with some to go back to Mother and the rent that won't leave much over, but that is usual."

He kissed me lightly and went off quite happy. As I watched him cycle up the road he turned his cycle round, waved his hand with a flourish, righted himself and was soon hidden from view behind a big belt of trees.

Four days later I received a letter from him. He had got to his mother's safely. The acetylene lamp had given trouble and he was in the dark for many miles. It had started to rain and he had got soaked to the skin long before he reached his parents' home. His leg was very bad and had been bleeding so was raw and he could not get his artificial leg on to even walk round the house. He did say that he realised now how foolish he had been to attempt to cycle such a long journey and now he had to face the journey back.

When I knew my father would not be at Woodlands I went to see Mother to ask her to lend me some money to send to David. I said that David's mother had little enough for herself and she certainly could not afford to feed David while he was there. I had to borrow for myself, too, to get some provisions. The pension due on the following Wednesday was already bespoken!

I sent the cash to David telling him it was borrowed and I hoped that he would make every effort to get back to Dilwyn.

When he did arrive, it was at midnight. He had had a wet journey and was soaked, cold and hungry, and very sorry for himself.

After a meal and dry pyjamas, he hopped up to bed and was too ill to get up for several days. I should have got the doctor to see him I know, but when I mentioned it he said, "We cannot afford the doctor's fees. He will charge five shillings for each visit and he won't be content to make one. Where do we get the money for several visits, I want to know?"

"You should have him, David. You are hot and feverish," I protested.

"No. Don't you dare get him. I will be all right."

I left the room and went downstairs. I didn't dare get the doctor with David in his present mood so later, when I felt he would be sleeping, I made a quick visit to my mother. Mother advised me not to push him to eat too much but to get extra milk and keep him on milk or anything light.

I did so and, after about four days, David decided to hop downstairs and sit in the chair. His leg was still very bad and he had to resort to his crutches for the remainder of the week.

It was a long time since he had done any work, in fact he had only done one week's work since we had been in the hop field in August.

I wanted to work, but there were only small cottages round me and the folks who lived in them were not any better off than we were; the only employment was for the farm labourers. In the village there were a few large houses but the owners could get all the domestic help they needed from the people who lived near. So to David and me there seemed no improving our position.

David proposed that we go back to live with his mother and Dad, but that was impossible as another brother had taken over our rooms.

David was silent all the afternoon as he stared moodily into the fire. We had chopped down an old apple tree that had died quite some time before and we now had the benefit of the wood whilst outside the weather was bitterly cold. We had had a little snow and we hoped we would see no more.

A night or two later it started to snow steadily after tea. David had been to 'our cabin in the pines' and he said, as he brushed his coat, "Snowing quite steady. If it keeps on it could be quite deep by morning. Better get some water in a pail and put it in the kitchen, save you going out to the well when you get up in the morning."

I did so. David said once when he peered down into the well that he supposed it could be about eighty foot deep.

Next morning I pulled the curtain aside to look through the window, then put it back quickly.

I got back into bed and told David the snow looked to be about a foot deep. I shuffled myself down close beside him and decided another hour would make no difference. By now we were both awake so we just lay and talked.

"Funny thing, dreams, do you know I dreamed that I died and I was all washed and had a clean shirt on. I was covered with a sheet right over my whole body, head and all and I seemed to stand by my body and stare at the sheet that I knew covered *me*."

"Oh shut up, David, for goodness' sake," I said.

"No, listen to me. I said that I was staring at the sheet that covered me and I took hold of it at the top and pulled it back to look at my face. I remember I said, 'Yes, it's me'. Then I looked, or tried to look at myself and although I knew I was there I could see nothing. I was standing by my body but I could see nothing of *me*."

David was very thoughtful and when I asked him what he was thinking about he said, "I wonder if there is anything in Spiritualism?"

"Does anyone know?" I said. "But you must agree when we were 'up home' and we used to go to the meetings, some funny things were told to people and they were told by strangers who did not know them and the things were correct. I mean, look how my uncle's place and my aunt were described and that woman who told me was right," I said.

"Hm. Yes," said David. "Well, I'll tell you what, if I die before you and I'm sure I will, if I die before you," he repeated, "I will come back to you if there is any coming back, I *will* come back to you and if you never see me then don't believe in it at all."

I did not like the turn of conversation.

"Yes. Let's make a pact. Whoever dies first must come back to the other, promise, and if the one who passes away doesn't appear then there is nothing to it, it's all bunk."

"All right. I agree. Let's forget the subject," I said.

★

From time to time, Mother would ask David to do a little job for her. He had told her long before that he would be most willing, if she needed help in any way, to come up to Woodlands, so mother would occasionally come down to our house and say, "David, are you busy?"

"No, Mam."

"Could you come and see to one of the locks on the door? It doesn't fasten very well."

And David would go back to Woodlands with her. Sometimes I think she invented little jobs for him.

She would say, "Come up tomorrow, David, I've one or two things want doing." And David would go.

I would ask when he came home about a couple of hours later, "What was the job Mother wanted done?"

"Nothing at all, really. She said sit down, and we talked. She always has some yarn about her young days to tell me and then she said, 'David, would you like a nice slice of ham off the shoulder hanging from the beam? I could do with one myself, I have eaten no breakfast as yet, so we'll have breakfast together.' She got the old frying pan out and I reached up and got down the ham and, with a couple of eggs for me and one for herself, we had a lovely meal. Nothing like home-cured bacon from your own pig," he ended wistfully.

Many meals David had with my mother. Sometimes there was a job to do, sometimes not, and I was grateful to Mother for her goodness to David, it made him less lonely.

Sometimes, too, when she came down to our house (not often, because Father would have been suspicious if the bacon was going down too quickly), she would bring a small piece of boiling bacon for us and, without her help (never asked for but always given), I would have found life much harder.

My little girls were now two and four years old, and now they had a little brother, a bonny child we named Robert John. He grew quickly: at ten months he was crawling round the house, and at sixteen months he was walking strongly, and was soon into everything. It was a relief when all three children could play out in the garden under the big fir tree.

The days were getting longer and now it was the end of

April. The trees with their blessed jacket of green leaves, the sun shining in a blue sky, the bees buzzing as they searched for pollen amongst the flowers in the front garden. Poor I may be, I thought, but life could be worse.

Except for his troublesome leg David seemed well. I would have liked to have mentioned to him how nice it would be if his parents were to come to visit us, but I could not stretch David's pension to feed seven of us and manage other expenses. I knew it would not occur to Mum-in-law to help out moneywise, so I refrained from saying anything.

A few weeks later we received a letter to say they would be coming down at the end of that week, so I set about preparing the spare room for them. Mother-in-law had baked the day before she came and had made some cakes to bring down for us all. I was really glad to see them. It was months since David had cycled to Abercynon and it really bucked him up now to have his parents with him. I knew he had been missing them very much, even though he had not said much about being so far away from them.

The weather remained good and David's parents stayed for three weeks. Father-in-law helped out by digging the part of the garden I had not managed to do and planted what seed needed to go into it. Otherwise, the old fellow would play with the children or go off on long walks by himself and, I suspected, call in the 'local' for the occasional half pint. No doubt his family had slipped the odd couple of shillings into his pocket when Mother-in-law wasn't looking. If it had not been for my desperate need of cash to pay the extra expenses I would have liked them to stay for always.

My father had been very cordial when we took the old people to his house and a few minutes after we arrived he had taken the big quart jug out to the barn and filled it to the brim with cider. After filling our glasses, he and the old chap would yarn about their young days. Father-in-law was from farming parents although he had left it many years. They had a lot in common, these two elderly men, and they ended their talk with remarks like, "Ah, those were good old days. You will never see those days again."

For my part I thought, a good job done. I could not see what was good about them. People were poorer *then* than in my lifetime and God knows we were poor enough and poverty was visible among the people of my village, but it must have been worse in my people's day.

My mother who came from a family of six children told me once that her father was a farm labourer so his wages were low and she herself used to go to the farm where her father worked to wash the dishes for the farmer's wife. She was so small she had to stand on a stool to reach the sink. She was six years old at the time.

I came to the conclusion that both Father and Father-in-law had forgotten the hardships of those days so long gone; life as we lived at that present day was totally different to their past days which were wrapped in a golden mist of memory that was a mirage.

Mother-in-law had received a letter from one of her daughters, who sent postal orders to cover the old people's fares home including payment for Mr Williams to take them the six miles into Leominster. I got the feeling that David's dad would have been happy to still stay on with us but Mother-in-law intended to take him back with her and I was glad.

I had had to borrow from my mother — two pounds — and I did not know how I was going to pay her back. When I saw her after the old people had departed I made a promise that if I did not manage to pay it back before the hop-picking season commenced we would pay her from what we earned then, and she was content with this.

Life seemed flat to David but Mother came down to say that a Mr Davies of Ventnor Farm needed some people to single out seedling mangolds. David decided to go at once to see if he could get taken on for the job. The farm was only a five-minute cycle ride away so he was gone only a short time and was pleased to tell me that he had been taken on. It seemed the pay was not by the day but, as the mangolds were planted in long, straight rows, the pay was for each row.

I said I would go with him to work too and he agreed. We packed some food and went off quite early the next day.

It seemed there were no other offers to take on the job so David and I took on clearing the seedlings until other help came. We did most of the big field in the days that followed. Mr Davies was quite pleased with our work and, each morning at about eleven-thirty, his wife brought us tea. If we were still there at three-thirty, she brought more tea. A couple of times she brought thin-cut home-made bread and butter with cakes.

The weather was good and David and I didn't mind the work at all, even though the bending down was back-aching, and made poor David's artificial leg rub on his stump but he would not give up. He did, however, slow our progress some. Even so, we finished the job and collected a nice bit of cash from which we were able to pay Mother the two pounds we owed.

Some time later, Mr Davies came to us. It seemed the hops were now needing to be tied to the poles. As the long vines cling like ivy to the poles and grow, thickly spreading great thongs out from the main stem, these soon becoming covered in golden flowers that grow like bunches of grapes, he offered us the job of tying the small stems to the poles. We said we would like to do the work if he would show us how. He did, and as before, Mrs Davies brought us jugs of tea and food to eat but we never counted on what she might give us and always took food in case one day she did not bring any. But Mrs Davies was very kind and gave us ample food so we took our packages home and used them for the next meal.

So that job ended with a nice bit of cash which we spent on clothes for us and the children but not a coat for me, my coat would have to do, perhaps until hop-picking time.

From time to time other jobs came from Mr Davies and I did not mind working in the fields too much. It brought extra cash to David's pension and things were better because we had a little more spending money.

And then the summer was with us and although no more jobs came our way from Mr Davies, we did not mind. We were glad to rest a while. Mr Davies had explained that now there was a 'lull' as things were growing but later on there would be other work if we wanted it. I was happy to leave that to the future.

Our own garden was doing well: potatoes, greens, carrots and onions were looking good and, although there was always some weeding to do and hoeing up of potatoes, we found time to go walking and for David to go swimming in the river. Permission was given him by our landlord, through whose grounds the river coursed; indeed his mill was kept going by the river and he was able to grind his own grain from the many acres he had seeded in corn, wheat and barley.

Our landlord had never offered work to David because he and his six sons did all the work on his place.

I had a bout of illness and I was in bed for nearly three weeks. Mrs Hellis, the landlord's wife, called to see me. I remember she brought me an egg-custard and sat a few minutes to talk with me. The conversation came round to farm life: whatever do people talk about except the way they live day by day? If you are a farmer's wife it is the work you are close to. If you are a pig owner or a poultry farmer or whatever else, it seems to be the biggest thing you talk of and these things can be very boring if you are not talking to someone in the same line as yourself.

I remember saying during the conversation, "You must work hard, having seven men to look after but you have a maid to help you and compensations — you own a big farm, you and Mr Hellis, and you have everything to enjoy, the love of your sons, all with you and you do not want for anything."

"Yes," said Mrs Hellis. "I have all these, but happiness very little. I have been ill as you know. I am not in the best of health and never will be again. Material gain is not everything. There are times when I have to jump between my sons and my husband when a particular one offends him, or he accuses one or other of not doing a job correctly. Life is not always easy."

I murmured something about being sorry.

She rose and went downstairs, after saying she would call again, but she never did call again.

During the summer David made many trips to the river. I would sit on the stone bridge and watch him.

August came and hop-picking time. I really looked forward to it but this time David was indifferent. He said he did not mind either way but every day if the weather was dry, we set off with the children after breakfast, and stayed until four o'clock.

One day, David said he was not feeling very good and I noticed he looked paler than usual. I suggested we stay home from the hop-fields. We had been to them for about six or seven days. But he refused to stay at home that morning. He said it was nothing and we could both come home if he felt worse.

The following day I did persuade him to stay at home and I went alone. When I returned he said he felt a lot better and I busied myself cooking dinner as always when we had been out all day.

He seemed to be all right in a day or two and he came to the field to finish up the second week. He was quiet and I knew he was not well. He said he had a pain in his chest which came and went.

The money was earned and spent on fuel: we were glad of a fire in the evenings when it was getting colder.

The days lengthened into November and one night David was taken very ill. I ran to a neighbour who lived a little way up the road and asked him to cycle to the village to fetch the doctor. By the time the doctor had arrived, David had passed away.

There had to be a postmortem, and it was found that David's heart had been in a bad way. David was twenty-seven years old. The frightful devastation of the war had finally taken its toll.

I sent a telegram to my parents-in-law and they came down in time for the funeral. I do not wish to dwell on death, the shock for his mother who was constantly in tears from the moment she arrived at our house. Father-in-law was restrained but I knew under his quiet exterior he grieved deeply.

My people-in-law knew I had had to accept my parents' help to cover funeral expenses and that I had to try for Government help to keep me. I could not afford the rent for our house any longer. My mother said I must give it up, and I gave a week's notice to Mr Hellis. She suggested my furniture could go into the big barn at Woodlands until it could be sold, and that I and the children could stay in the spare room there until I decided what was best to do.

A letter came a day or two later instructing me to return my husband's two artificial legs to Roehampton and postage would be refunded. The legs were packed and posted and I duly received a postal order for two shillings for the cost of the postage.

I had no alternative but to go and live once again at Woodlands. I set about packing my china and other goods.

It was only when I had finally left my little cottage which I had so loved, and had stacked the furniture in my father's barn to await its sale, that I realised fully what had happened to me.

David and I had been married for seven years. We had been more or less happy. I had three beautiful, tiny children who were now without a father. And in my purse I had three shillings — all the money I possessed in the world. I was going to be very lonely. I remember sitting out in my father's barn and crying until I could cry no more.

I could not look upon Woodlands as my home. But I made up my mind that tears were no help and that I must look to the future. I was going, somehow or other, to depend only on myself. I would get myself a job . . . as the motto in the cracker had said: 'Look forward to tomorrow'.